"ALL YOU HAVE [ ] *P9-EEE-121*
YOUR OWN KINKINESS . . . IF YOU
CENSOR THINGS OUT IN DEFERENCE
TO SOME FEAR OF EXPOSURE, FEAR
OF WHAT YOUR FAMILY, YOUR
HUSBAND, YOUR LOVER, OR YOUR
FRIENDS MAY THINK, THEN YOU'RE
GOING TO LOSE AUTHENTICITY. . . .
IT'S ESPECIALLY HARD FOR WOMEN.
MEN ARE AFRAID, TOO, OF COURSE,
BUT IN WOMEN THE FEAR OF
SELF-EXPOSURE IS EVEN MORE."
—Erica Jong, in the interview in this book

The poems in this dazzling volume are a form of art-ful self-exposure—one of the most naked self-exposures a woman has ever achieved. In so revealing herself, Erica Jong has succeeded in revealing all people, with the wit, wisdom and whiplash honesty that make her one of the most exciting writers in the world today.

HERE COMES
& OTHER POEMS

"WILL MAKE LITERARY HISTORY!"
—*Henry Miller*

Works by Erica Jong

Fruits & Vegetables (poems) 1971

Half-Lives (poems) 1973

Fear of Flying (a novel) 1973-1974

Loveroot (poems) 1975

Here Comes & Other Poems 1975

ERICA JONG

HERE COMES
& OTHER POEMS

ORIGINALLY PUBLISHED AS

Fruits & Vegetables

AND

Half-Lives

*Including an interview
with the author
and selected prose*

A SIGNET BOOK

NEW AMERICAN LIBRARY

TIMES MIRROR

ACKNOWLEDGMENTS
Fruits & Vegetables:
  The following poems were first published in *Poetry:*
  "Touch"; "Narcissus, Photographer"; "Books";
  "Where It Begins." "The Heidelberg Landlady" first
  appeared in *The Beloit Poetry Journal* as "The
  Landlady," and has been slightly revised. Parts of
  "Fruits & Vegetables" and "The Objective Woman" first
  appeared in *Twen* (West Germany) in German
  translation.

  Other poems were previously published in the
  following periodicals: *Aphra, Intro, #3, The Beloit
  Poetry Journal, Mademoiselle,* and *The Southern Review.*
  Special thanks to Grace Darling.

  *Grateful acknowledgment is made for use of the
  following:*
  One line from "First Meditation," © 1955 by
  Theodore Roethke, from *The Collected Poems
  of Theodore Roethke.* Reprinted by permission of
  Doubleday & Company, Inc.
  One line from "Blue" by Rafael Alberti from *The
  Poems of Rafael Alberti,* translated by Mark Strand.
  Reprinted by permission of Las Americas Publishing
  Company of New York City.

(The following pages constitute an extension of this copyright page.)

I am grateful to the Creative Artists Public Service Program of the New York State Council on the Arts, and to the Poetry Society of America for grants which helped in the completion of this book.

Thanks also to Grace Darling Griffin, Patricia Goedicke Robinson, Robert Phillips, Aaron Asher, Norma Klein, Rosellen Brown, Anita Gross, and Louis Untermeyer.

Contents

Interview
with Erica Jong*

NYQ: How do you start a poem?

ERICA JONG: That's a very difficult question. My way of writing has changed considerably in the past few years. At this point, I usually get a first line. I don't know where that first line comes from and I don't know who says it to me. It may be the Muse. (I really believe in the Muse, by the way.) But the process seems to be that I get a line and write it down as quickly as I can and generally from that I allow things to build. I follow the images one after the other seemingly automatically. That doesn't mean that my poems are not revised or edited, but they come in a very mysterious way. Almost by dictation.

I didn't always write this way, however. When I was in college I wrote in a much more premeditated manner. I would struggle from one line to the next, poring over a rhyming dictionary, counting out the meter on my fingers. Although I now write very freely, I'm conscious of the oral qualities of the poetry and of the rhythm. Also, I don't let everything stand. The second draft is written extremely critically. Most of the process consists of striking out the crap—the bad lines.

But I can't tell you where my first line comes from.

*This craft interview first appeared in *New York Quarterly*, Number 16. It is reprinted in *The Craft of Poetry*, edited by William Packard, copyright 1974, Doubleday & Co., Inc. It was conducted in Erica Jong's home in June, 1973, and has been slightly revised for publication in the present volume.

I do know that I recognize Osip Mandelstam's description of the kind of foretrembling which precedes writing a poem. It's a weird kind of excitement which feels somewhat like sexual tension and somewhat like anxiety. It's as if an aura exists around you—and you know you're going to write a poem that day. The real question of beginning is when you get the hook into the poem, and that hook is the first line. It may not always *remain* the first line. It may become the last line, or it may drop out of the poem altogether, but it's the line that starts your imagination working.

NYQ: Do you usually finish the poem in one day or work on it for a while?

EJ: It depends. Some poems are finished in one day. Others take years. Sometimes the process is merely a question of refining, and sometimes you have to grow into a poem. I have a poem which is just beginning now, and I haven't the faintest idea when I'll finish it. There are two lines that really live. Two images. But they haven't grown into a poem yet.

NYQ: It's working?

EJ: It's there working, yes. I'm reminded of the motto Kafka had over his writing desk—"Wait." And it's true. You're not always conscious of working on a poem. And then it happens. It erupts like a volcano. Your imagination is working all the time in a subterranean way. And when it comes time for you to write the poem, the whole thing explodes.

NYQ: What about ideas for a novel—is it a whole section, a chapter . . . ?

EJ: *Fear of Flying* was written in such a funny way that it's difficult to describe the process. I had been working for years on sections of it and I had attempted two earlier novels that I didn't finish. I had been collecting autobiographical fragments, fantasies, character sketches, ideas. When the framing device for this book—the trip across Europe—occurred to me, I suddenly found a way to make a coherent story out of materials which had been obsessing me for quite some time.

NYQ: One of the questions we were going to ask you was about the Muse. Because you do mention her in a very specific personal way sometimes.

EJ: How do you mean?

NYQ: You talk about her in a very familiar way as if you met her and she's right there beside you. Could you talk about it?

EJ: Well, I used to think that all this talk about the Muse was a lot of bullshit. But I was wrong. I'm convinced that there are powers we cannot find names for. Maybe the Muse is really the same as the collective unconscious. I don't think it matters. Maybe the Muse is one's own unconscious which connects with the collective unconscious. Or maybe the Muse is a supernatural being. But I think there are forces we have no way of scientifically codifying, and inspiration is one of them. Why is it that at a given moment in your life certain elements come together and fuse in a way that makes a poem or that allows you to write a novel you've been dreaming for years?

NYQ: So you call it the Muse?

EJ: Yes, but that's just one of many possible terms. That quality of inspiration, that sudden chill, the thing that makes your hair stand on end . . . I don't know what else to call it. You see, I think part of being a poet is learning how to tap your inner resources. Probably poets are born, not made. But the training of a poet consists in learning how to tap that secret part of yourself which connects with the communal unconscious. So you spend a lot of time imitating other people's poems. Writing on subjects that, let's say, aren't of interest to you but were of interest to the poets you admire. You're learning your craft. But what you're really learning during those years of apprenticeship is how to explore yourself. And when that happens—I've said this in my poetry seminar about a million times—when craft and the exploration of self come together, that's when you become a poet. All the stuff you produced before that was derivative apprenticeship work. And you usually know it when that point arrives.

NYQ: One of the quotations you had in your article "The Artist as Housewife"* was "Everyone has talent, what is rare is the courage to follow the talent to the dark place where it leads." What has helped you the most to go into those dark places?

EJ: I had to learn to trust myself. I had to learn to trust that part of my mind which had the potential of being original. I think lots of things helped. Getting older and having more confidence in my own voice. The other thing (unfashionable as it's become) was psychoanalysis. Artists tend to be afraid of it. They think they'll lose their creativity. But what analysis teaches you is how to surrender yourself to your fantasies. How to dive down into those fantasies. If you can do it on the couch—and not all people can do it on the couch either—then you may learn to trust the unconscious. To follow its meandering course. Not to look for a goal. As in an analytic session where you begin meandering. "Oh, this doesn't make any sense at all. I'm saying X. I'm saying Y." And then at the end of the session you discover that it does make sense. It makes more sense than "rational" discourse. There are a lot of dreadful analysts around—just as there are a lot of incompetents in any other profession. But about two percent of them are artists, and understand artists. I was also lucky to have some teachers who knew where I was going. And who encouraged me when my poetry began to take the inner direction. Stanley Kunitz and Mark Strand, for

*"The Artist as Housewife" appears on page 255.

example, with whom I studied at Columbia from 1969 to 1970. Earlier, at Barnard, Robert Pack had been my poetry teacher and had taught me the importance of craft, of being able to write a creditable sonnet or a mock epic in heroic couplets (before attempting free verse). As a correspondent, critic, and spiritual grandfather, Louis Untermeyer has also been a great inspiration to me.

NYQ: You mention voice in that same article. You say that the poet's main problem is to "raise a voice." How did you find your voice and how do you suggest a poet find his voice? Going into himself?

EJ: Well, I remember my gradual realization that the person I was in life and the person I was in my poems were not the same. When I wrote poetry I assumed a kind of poet-role. It probably came out of some old grade-school notion of what a poet is. We all have that and it somehow stands in our way. I realized that in life I was a clown, alternately very solemn and serious—and at other times, kidding around wildly. But I never had allowed that range in my work. I had always been attracted to satire, and even in my high school and college poems, I had tried to write satire. But it was a kind of formal satire written in imitation of Alexander Pope. It wasn't really open and spontaneous. I had to learn to let spontaneity into my poems.

NYQ: You speak frequently of the need for authenticity. Is the need for authenticity the need for trusting yourself?

EJ: Yes, because all you have to write out of is your own kinkiness, the idiosyncrasies of your personality, the special spectacles through which you view the world. If you censor those things out in deference to some fear of exposure, fear of what your family, your husband, your lover, or your friends may think, then you're going to lose authenticity. When you write, you're not writing for an outer social world that approves or does not approve. Writing is for that inner place, that inner place in other people, too. That's what I mean by authenticity. And it's very hard to get past this obsession with trying to please. It's especially hard for women. Men are afraid, too, of course, but in women the fear of self-exposure is even more cultivated.

NYQ: Many of your poems refer to specific people who seem to be in your life. There is a poem called "Chinese Food," for example, where there are specific people by name. And in some of your recent poems you mention your mother. How do you deal with these poems that are maybe biographical in one way, maybe nonliteral in other ways? How do you deal with this issue of speaking from your voice and also that of other people?

EJ: I don't think that any of the people in my poems are real people in a strict biographical sense. Obviously, they are people frozen at certain moments in time. My real biographical mother is not merely like the mother in that poem. And she would be the first to say so.

I don't think that adherence to biographical incident is a fair criterion by which to measure a poem. There's a wonderful quote from Jerzy Kosinski which I used in *Fear of Flying.* He says that you can't have such a thing as straight autobiography or confessional writing because even if you *try* to write down literally what you remember, memory *itself* fictionalizes and orders and structures. Even if you make a film or a tape, you have to edit it, and in so doing, you put a controlling intelligence around it. It ceases to be the same as biography.

What you're talking about in my poems is that they refer to—yes, I have a mother—everybody has a mother —I could have written twelve other poems about my mother in different incarnations and I probably *will* as time goes on. But I don't see the people in those poems as "real" people. The Chinese food poem mentions people who were present at a given dinner. But those people aren't really depicted. And I don't see my poems as confessional at all. I see them as "structures made to accommodate certain feelings." (The phrase Kosinski uses.) Obviously they come out of my life. But then all the poets' poems come out of their lives.

If the people in the poems were just people in my own life, and hadn't any universal meaning, nobody else could connect with those poems. They would be so personal that they would mean nothing to anybody but *me*. That's why I think the term confessional poetry is an absolute misnomer. I don't think there *is* such a thing as confessional poetry.

NYQ: One term you do use is "author" in the sense of authority. What would you say is the author's particular responsibility as an author writing today?

EJ: When I talk about authority, what I mean is: You are the person where the buck stops. You are responsible for what you write. You cannot write a book in committee, nor with a certain editor, publisher, or reviewer in mind. Writing is one of the few professions left where you take all the responsibility for what you do. It's really dangerous and ultimately destroys you as a writer if you start thinking about responses to your work or what your audience needs. That's what I mean by authority. And that's why I say again and again to my poetry seminar: "Don't even listen to *me*. We're offering criticisms of your poems and we're saying—'Okay, that line works, that line doesn't work.' But if you want to ignore it, go ahead and ignore it because learning to be a writer means learning to ignore people's advice when it's bad." You have to reach that place in yourself where you know your own sound, your own rhythm, your own voice. That's what it's all about. You'll find that with many great authors of the past, their strengths and weaknesses are so intertwined that one can't unravel them. A contemporary author like Doris Lessing is a good example of this. She can be incredibly hard to read, almost boring at times. And yet she's a great writer. It's the very heaviness of her writing, the way she works out a detailed portrait of a society that makes her so good. How could an editor sit down with *The Golden Notebook* and excise passages? God knows there are sections of it that are very heavy going. Yet the strengths of the book and the faults are so interwoven that editing it would be impossible. You can't make *The Golden Notebook* into an E. M. Forster or Elizabeth Bowen novel. It's a different animal. You try to refine your work as much as you can. But ultimately you have to say: "I am I. I am the author." That's what I want everyone in my seminar to learn eventually.

NYQ: You mentioned earlier some of the problems of being a woman poet. In your article "The Artist as Housewife," you said, "Being an artist of any sex is such a difficult business that it seems almost ungenerous and naïve to speak of the special problems of the woman artist . . ." What are those special problems?

EJ: There are many. Despite the fact that we've had Sappho, Emily Dickinson, Jane Austen, the Brontës, Colette, Virginia Woolf, etc., etc., etc., there is still the feeling that women's writing is a lesser class of writing, that to write about what goes on in the nursery or the bedroom is not as important as what goes on in the battlefield, that to write about relationships between men and women is not as important as writing about a moonshot. Somehow there's a feeling that what women know about is a lesser category of knowledge. It's women's fiction, women's poetry, or something like that. Women are more than half the human race, and yet since the culture has always been male-dominated, the things men are interested in are thought to be of greater importance than the things women are interested in. Also, there is still a tremendous condescension toward women in reviewing. Whenever people tote up the lists of the greatest writers now writing, you get the same male names over and over. You don't get Eudora Welty, Doris Lessing, Mary McCarthy, Adrienne Rich, Muriel Rukeyser, Anne Sexton. Why? There is a kind of patriarchal prejudice which infuses our whole culture. I think it is not *always* malicious on the part of men—it's often purely unconscious. The psychological reasons behind this are many. Probably womb-envy—that most unrecognized phenomenon—plays a significant part. Since the majority of psychologists and anthropologists have been male, they've been reluctant to recognize it. Men have the feeling that women can create life in their bodies, therefore how *dare* they create art?

NYQ: Do you think women writers have more difficulty getting published because of this?

EJ: It's hard to generalize because women are being published now for faddish reasons. Let's just say women don't have difficulty being published. But they do have difficulty being taken *seriously* as writers. Certain kinds of writing are almost exclusively done by women—Gothic romances, children's books. Yet being published is quite a different thing from being accorded respect as an *artist*. Secondhand bookstores are strewn with books which were published and forgotten.

NYQ: You mentioned women writers. Do you find it more often that women are reviewed as women than as writers?

EJ: I've never seen a review of a woman writer in which her sex was not mentioned in some way. And frequently reviewers do things like comment on appearance. Carolyn Kizer was reviewed (I think in

Time or *Newsweek*) as "the Mae West of the poetry world" or some crap like that. There are many good-looking male poets and people don't go around saying, "Isn't W. S. Merwin a cutie?" I mean, he's very handsome. Richard Wilbur is very handsome. Mark Strand is very handsome. I hope I haven't left anybody out. But people don't talk about that in reviews of men. With women they *always* talk about it. And if a woman's ugly, they harp on that too. Did you see that reference to Gertrude Stein's "fat ankles" in *The Times* a few weeks ago? It's as if you're a piece of meat. Besides condescension and not being taken seriously, there's that awful category of "woman poet." *Women's* conflicts—as if they weren't applicable to *all* of us.

NYQ: Now when you go in to your workroom and begin to work, and you're a poet and also a woman, what special kind of traps do you have to look out for because of this scene in terms of your craft? In terms of your voice?

EJ: As I said in "The Artist as Housewife" article, I went for a long time not dealing with my feelings about being a woman, because I had never really seen it done before. In college I read Auden, Yeats, Eliot, and Dylan Thomas, and imitated a male voice. I didn't think of it as a male voice, I thought of it as a *poet's* voice, but it didn't always deal with the things that I wanted to deal with. Perhaps the reason Sylvia Plath was so important to my generation of young women was that she wrote about being a woman and she wrote about its negative side. She dealt with birth, menstruation—all the things that male poets don't deal with. So she liberated us. Now I think we can go beyond that. We don't *always* have to write about female rage.

NYQ: Do you have any work habits? Isadora writes in the nude. Do you have work habits like this?

EJ: I *don't* always write in the nude. Anyway that's not a work habit.

NYQ: Do you have any—certain papers—in longhand?

EJ: I write in longhand and I write very fast. I like to have a pen that flows rapidly because when the words start coming they come so fast that my handwriting is virtually illegible. I can't compose on a typewriter, although my second draft is typed. It gets pasted into my notebook side by side with the scrawled first draft and I refine it from there.

NYQ: Do you keep a journal?

EJ: I don't really have time, though I would love to. I've kept journals at many times in my life, starting from when I was about thirteen or fourteen. But it's boring and contrived to keep a journal every day. Better to write as the mood strikes. But I don't even have time to do that except on rare occasions. Writing a novel, writing poems, writing letters to many correspondents, trying to keep notes on poems that come to mind—there just isn't time to keep a journal. Also you use up the energy that might go into poems.

NYQ: Do you write every day—your poems, your novel— Do you write at a set time?

EJ: Writing a novel is a very tough discipline. Poems can be written in spurts, irregularly. I sometimes write ten poems at once. But of those ten, perhaps one third will eventually be published. With a novel it's a whole different thing. You sit down every morning and push that pen across the page, and you have to get from one point to another. You know that you have to move your character to a certain city and out again and you must do it that day whether you feel like it or not. You don't always *start out* inspired, but as you work your way into the scene, things start happening. You begin pushing that pen along, and then maybe after two hours you're really going. Things you hadn't expected are happening on the page. There's such a hell of a lot of sheer plugging. Sometimes you write chapters and chapters and wind up discarding them. But you plod along day after day. You have to get up every morning at eight o'clock (or whenever) and sit down for at least three or four hours.

By the way, I think that you can be a writer with four hours a day to write. Although you may need two hours of warm-up time before, and two hours of wind-down time afterward.

NYQ: We were talking about serving your apprenticeship as a poet and becoming a poet.

EJ: There was something I wanted to add about that. You have to find that place in yourself where you have great control, yet great freedom. Control over your craft so it's almost automatic. And at the same time great freedom to deal with unconscious material. That's the point at which you become a poet. Both things are not always operating at optimum pitch, however. You may sit down in the morning and feel that you're going to write a poem, but the poem you produce may be just a warm-up for some other unwritten poem.

NYQ: Do you use special exercises like free association exercises or games to get you going?

EJ: No, I don't, but sometimes I read.

NYQ: Which poets?

EJ: Lately I've been reading a lot of Neruda. God help me for saying that. Every time you mention a name in an interview, you get haunted by that name from then on. Critics will clobber me with "influenced by Neruda"—but the reason I read him is that he shows me the possibilities of the imagination. I love the way he associates from one image to the next. It gets my mind going. But when I write, I write poems very different from the ones I've been reading. I may read a poem by Neruda that deals with death. But that doesn't mean I'm going to write a poem about death.

NYQ: What do you do when you are plunging underwater and you hit a block, when you can't write any-more, when the poem doesn't mesh and when you sense it's a block rather than just being finished for that day?

EJ: You leave the poem in your notebook and come back to it eventually. Months or years later you may see it very clearly. I save all my notebooks, and from time to time when I don't know what I'm going to write, I read them over and find the first line of a poem which I started but couldn't finish and sometimes I'm able to finish it. Nothing you write is ever lost to you. At some other level your mind is working on it.

NYQ: Are there times when you can't write anything? How do you get around them?

EJ: One of the happy things about writing both prose and poetry is that you always have something to do. We have a funny idea in this country about over-specialization. Lately I've been writing poems, articles, and prose fiction and it's been a good combination for me. Obviously you're not going to be at the peak of inspiration every day. And if you're not writing poems, why should it be dishonorable to write an article?

NYQ: Then you don't have problems with blocks?

EJ: Not at the moment. God knows I had lots of them in the past, and may have again in the future. Knock on wood.

NYQ: In your article "The Artist as Housewife" you wrote about the willingness to finish things being a good measure as to whether one was adult or not. Could you talk about this willingness to finish work as a special problem of the artist?

EJ: I went for years not finishing anything. Because, of course, when you finish something, you can be judged. My poems used to go through 360 drafts. I had poems which were rewritten so many times that I suspect it was just a way of avoiding sending them out.

NYQ: You can see it very clearly now.

EJ: When I look at some of those drafts, I realize that beyond a certain point I wasn't improving anything. I was just obsessing. I was afraid to take risks.

NYQ: Is this more of a problem with women, do you think?

EJ: It's hard to generalize, but since women are encouraged not to have responsibility for their own lives, I suppose they *do* have more of a problem in this respect. Of course throughout history there have always been women who didn't give in to the demand that they remain children. Nevertheless, a woman's time tends to be more fragmented. (I can just hear all the male poets I know who have office jobs screaming and yelling.) But perhaps it's not a problem of sheer time; perhaps it has more to do with not trusting yourself. Also women want to find men they admire and look up to. And that's very dangerous.

NYQ: What started you writing?

EJ: I don't remember a time when I didn't write. As a kid I used to keep journals and notebooks. I wrote stories and illustrated them. I never *said* I wanted to be a writer, but I always wrote. Still, it was hard to make the step of saying "I'm a writer" before I had published. I would shuffle my feet and look down at the floor. After my first book was accepted for publication, I began to think "Gee, I'm a poet." Talk about being other-directed.

NYQ: You mentioned once that your early poems were in traditional verse form and that you came rather late to free writing. What would you say about that kind of classical training for a poet?

EJ: I think it's tremendously important. You get letters from people saying: "I love to write poetry and I have twenty-six manuscripts of poetry in my desk drawer but I never read poetry." The country is full of "poets" who have never bought a book of poetry. If every person who sends poems to magazines would just buy one slim volume of verse, poets would not be starving. I've spent years reading poetry. I went to graduate school and read ancient and modern poetry, imitated Keats, imitated Pope, imitated Browning . . . Learning is good for a poet as long as she doesn't become a professional scholar.

NYQ: Can you write prose and poetry simultaneously?

EJ: For the first six months when I was writing my novel, I wrote poems simultaneously. But then when I got very deep into *Fear of Flying* (when I got past the 200-page point) it really took over—and from that point on, I couldn't write poetry. Many of the poems in *Half-Lives* were written the year before *Fruits & Vegetables* was published, and many of them were written the following year. Some of them were written during the time I was beginning the novel. But fiction takes over your life. The final section in *Fear of Flying* (the chapter where Isadora is alone in Paris, abandoned in the hotel room) nearly did me in. Although the scene itself was totally invented, I felt that *I* was abandoned in that hotel room. It was ghastly. Then I spent months writing chapters which never found their way into the book at all. The ending was finally rewritten at least seven times. The last chapter, which is now about six pages long, was rewritten so many times you wouldn't believe it. And I finally wound up with a minimal amount of words but just the *right* sort of indeterminate feeling I wanted. I had written it every other way imaginable.

NYQ: Other endings?

EJ: Yes. And I won't tell you what they are.

NYQ: One of the last poems in *Half-Lives* has long prose poem sections in it. Was that a coincidence or were you working on *Fear of Flying* then?

EJ: I think I'm going to do more of that. Prose and poetry intermingled. It didn't really have to do with my writing a novel, but I'm very interested in mixed forms. Even *Fear of Flying* has a few poems in it.

NYQ: You mentioned that you raised your own consciousness as an artist while your home was in Germany. Then you mentioned just now that Paris became a locale for you. Generally speaking, how do you feel your locale affects the way you work as a poet?

EJ: The German experience was complicated because it made me suddenly realize I was Jewish. I had been raised as an atheist by cosmopolitan parents who didn't care about religion, and living in Germany gave me a sense of being Jewish and potentially a victim. That opened up my poetry. I wrote a whole sequence called "The Heidelberg Poems," some of which were published in the *Beloit Poetry Journal* under my maiden name. They dealt with a kind of primal terror and with being a victim of Nazism. After writing those poems, I was able to explore my own feelings and emotions in a way I hadn't before. The experience wasn't pleasant, but it was a deepening one.

NYQ: How do you find the New York locale as a place for a working poet?

EJ: I must say that I don't give a lot of importance to locale despite what I just said about Germany. At that point in my life it was important to be in touch with those feelings of terror. But I don't think it matters where the hell you write. You write where you are. You write from your head. You don't write in Paris or London or Heidelberg. But perhaps I'm too harsh about this because I'm not a landscape poet. I write about my own inner geography.

But there are other things in New York that are very distracting. Too many parties. Too many telephone calls. Too many people. Yet when I found myself last summer at Cape Cod sitting alone for hours and listening to the ocean, I would call long distance to New York because it was too quiet. I couldn't stand it.

Still, I do think it's kind of phony when young people say: "I'm going off to Europe with my notebook in my hand. I will be inspired by the fountains of Rome or sitting in a café in Paris." What crap. (I did it, too, of course.) You write best in a place where you're comfortable and can stack papers on the floor. But beyond that, locale doesn't matter.

NYQ: When you talk about that room of your own, what do you mean particularly?

EJ: I mean a place where you can close the door, make a mess if necessary, and nobody bothers you. My mother, who is a very talented painter, never had a room of her own, had to set up her easel in the living room and put away her paints if people were coming over. That's very destructive, especially for a woman. Staking out your territory is the big definition of identity that you win within your family or with the person you live with. That in itself is a very important struggle. When you can say to the people you live with: "This is the place where I work," then part of the battle of your identity as an artist has been fought. And in a very tangible way.

NYQ: Could you comment on the question of the selfishness of the artist to demand time and space—the whole question of selfishness as a working condition.

EJ: We all suffer about this. If you want to have human relationships, it's very hard to say: "Now I am closing the door to work." But the people you live with have to be aware that you are not shutting them out and it's not a rejection of them. It's very hard to be a writer because it means taking seriously your own nightmares and daydreams. If you're a young un- published writer and you're closing yourself in a room, neglecting other people, it seems very selfish. Almost like masturbation. But you have to believe in yourself. It helps a lot if the people you live with respect what you're doing. My husband respected my work at first more than I respected it. He'd say: "You have to work." And I'd say: "Help, let me out!"

NYQ: Like Colette.

EJ: Well, not quite. Willy locked her in a room to turn out these Claudine novels. He was exploiting her financially.

NYQ: You once suggested writing a poem from a dream and dream images. How do you feel about using dream material.

EJ: Again, that has to do with total self-surrender. But I've always found that if you try to use *literal* dreams in your work they're very boring. It's like waking up in the morning and trying to tell your dream to somebody at the breakfast table. Fascinating to you but to the other person, incredibly tedious. So when you use dream images in poems you have to be selective as with any other poetic images.

NYQ: How do you feel about the use of drugs to get into a poem?

EJ: I've never been able to do it. With pot, all I want to do is sit around and eat. I don't have any interest in writing whatsoever. Alcohol also makes me incapable of writing. Hashish is like pot—only more so. And I've never tried LSD. I tend to think that drugs are useless to writers. But that may just be because I have not been able to use them. I think that when you write you need a combination of great control and great abandonment. What the drug gives you is great abandonment, but the control goes all to hell.

NYQ: What special things do you want to happen, do you think can happen in a workshop?

EJ: One of the best things that happened to me when I was in a workshop at the School of the Arts at Columbia was that I met a lot of other poets. They turned me on to lots of books. Also I got feedback on my work. I met people I could exchange poems with. And from time to time somebody would say something that made me think hard. I don't think a workshop teaches you how to be a writer, but it serves its purpose in indirect ways.

NYQ: What assignments do you find helpful for beginning writers, thinking over your own workshops?

EJ: That's hard. Some students come to you with too much freedom. They cannot censor themselves at all. For those you have to stress craft. Other students come to you so hung up on craft that they have absolutely no freedom. For them you stress freedom. What works for one student doesn't work for another. So to say something in an interview like: "Craft is the most important thing" is misleading.

NYQ: Did the workshops help you in your own writing?

EJ: Yes. But that was because I worked with different poets. It's dangerous to have only one mentor. What you'll do is pick up all that poet's prejudices and imitate them. It's much better to study with a variety of people.

But the most important education you get is on your own. It's like what Rilke said in *Letters to a Young Poet:* "There's only one way—go in to yourself." You learn in solitude from reading other writers. And from writing and writing and writing. A workshop can accelerate that process, but the basic learning you do is alone.

NYQ: You've run workshops for high school students and for adults. What do you find happening in the two age groups when you get started?

EJ: It's really not all that different except that (as you'd expect) a high school student is less sophisticated. I honestly think it's a rare high school student who has her or his own voice. You must have a certain amount of maturity to be a poet. Seldom do sixteen-year-olds know themselves well enough. You can work a lot with students at that level, but it's really preparatory work. I go into shock when I see a South American poet with a first book at the age of nineteen. In North America we tend to have a prolonged adolescence. We're more likely to publish around the age of thirty. I think it was Neruda's *Twenty Poems of Love and a Song of Despair* which was published when he was nineteen or twenty. But in South America they tend to grow up faster than we do. It must be the heat.

NYQ: It may have to do with the competitiveness of the publishing business.

EJ: I don't know anything about publishing in South America. But I do know from my experience with other writers that most North Americans don't come into their maturity until they are at least twenty-five. I hate making generalizations like that because I can see people writing it down and saying—Ah, until I'm twenty-five . . . There are always millions of exceptions.

I used to sit around reading books and comforting myself. Virginia Woolf didn't publish her first book till she was past thirty. Katherine Anne Porter was thirty-three when she published her first short story. I would obsessively collect such facts. If I had known someone in high school or college and saw something published by him before I was published, it threw me into an envious rage. Being unpublished is so painful.

NYQ: How do you feel about publishing? Do you feel it's important for a poet to be published?

EJ: Obviously if you write, you want to communicate with other people. To say that you don't is a lie. But I'm not sure that publication always reflects quality. Magazines buy poems for very strange reasons. And for a young poet to determine whether or not his work is successful, dependent on whether or not he gets published, is a very dangerous business. I think the best poems in my first book never got taken by magazines. My name was unknown, so nobody cared. Also, many of them were long, and lots of magazines use poems as fillers.

NYQ: What about sending out?

EJ: Yes, I think it's helpful to send work out, depending on what kind of reaction you have when it's rejected. If you take that as a final judgment, it's dangerous. But if you do it in a kind of lighthearted way (who does it in a lighthearted way? Nobody!), it's okay. You must realize that people who accept or reject your poems are not always infallible.

NYQ: You can be affected by the recognition after publication.

EJ: I was helped by the freedom it gave me. You see, I was one of these people who was very hung up and insecure. I had all kinds of blocks and problems and didn't believe I was a poet, so when people began saying to me: "Hey, you really can write," it gave me a lot more confidence and it made writing easier. But this is tremendously individual. I think for somebody else, it might be ruination. I am extremely self-critical and don't publish everything I write. I sometimes get requests from little magazines which say: Send us anything you have. And my theory is I'm *not* going to publish anything I have. If I publish a poem I want it to be something I care about.

NYQ: What about poetry readings? How do they affect your own writing?

EJ: They've made me very aware of the rhythms of my poetry.

NYQ: Would you rather have your poetry read on a page or heard as a poem?

EJ: Both. I like people to hear me read because I think that they understand the poetry better. When I read, I feel I'm giving life to the poem.

NYQ: Does this desire to have your poetry read influence some of the forms you use like the list poems or the poems where a certain word or phrase is repeated?

EJ: No, it isn't premeditated. I do think my poetry has a kind of sound quality. Very often it uses repetition. But I think that poetry by *nature* is a form brought alive by the human voice.

NYQ: Could you comment on what you think poetry is?

EJ: It's voice music. Ancient poetry was all produced for that purpose. And that's still a very strong tradition. I don't think it was produced by the "reading scene" of the late sixties and early seventies. This was the ancient function of poetry. We haven't created a tradition—we've just rediscovered it. There was a period in American poetry in the forties and fifties when verse was very difficult, involuted, and meant to be studied and read on the page. That was partly the influence of the New Criticism. Since tight academic verse was being written by a certain segment of American poets, those of us who went to college at the time thought that to be the nature of poetry. On the contrary, that period was actually rather aberrant. Poetry has more often been a spoken thing than a difficult metaphysical puzzle. When I write, I always hear the voice in my head. I'm baffled that there is even a question about it.

Still, since we're into definitions of poetry, I think I ought to add that condensation is essential. Images are important to me because the image is a kind of emotional shorthand. Poetic language must be rhythmic, fresh, interesting language, but it must also be condensed and pack a lot of meaning into a little space.

NYQ: Are there any contemporary poets that you feel particularly close to?

EJ: I could name them, but then the people I hadn't named would wonder why I hadn't named them and it would only be because they hadn't popped into my head. There are so many.

NYQ: Do you think there are many good poets around?

EJ: I think we're living at a time of great renaissance for poets.

NYQ: You mentioned once that when you were a beginning poet it helped to get together with small groups
of poets and read work in progress. Do you continue
to do that?

EJ: I have a number of friends who are writers and who
read my work. There were specific people who were
very important to me when I was putting together my
first published book. I used to get together with Norma
Klein and Rosellen Brown and Patricia Goedicke. I
think it's very important to find friends whose prejudices you know. And who care about you and your
work and will be honest with you. You must share
enough values with them so that you can trust each
other. Finding such friends might be the most important
thing a young poet does. You need a critic, but it can't
be just *anybody*. The idea of sending your work to
a stranger is perhaps not such a good idea. You need
somebody whose prejudices you know.

NYQ: There must be a need for criticism. So many manuscripts come into the *Quarterly* with requests for
criticism.

EJ: Yes, and it's so hard to honor such a request because
you don't know the person. And often you don't
know what kind of psychological problems are going
on behind the request. It's not as simple as it looks. If
you write a critical letter to somebody, you may
absolutely destroy that person. Or make him furious.

NYQ: Do you get manuscripts from strangers?

EJ: Yes. Everybody does. It's just impossible to deal with.
You don't know how this person is going to react to
what you say or what you may be stirring up. Also,
if you answered them all, you'd never write a single
poem again. You'd become a full-time letter-writer. I
know. I spent months of my life doing just that.
Finally I gave up.

NYQ: Do you have a favorite poem?

EJ: How can you have a favorite poem? Your favorite

poem is always the one you just wrote. The others are not quite real to you. I read *Half-Lives* now (those poems were finished about a year ago and other people tell me they're enjoying them), but I can't enjoy them. They seem very remote from me now.

NYQ: What will your next book of poems be like?

EJ: It's too early to tell. I think I will do some more combinations of prose and poetry like "From the Country of Regrets." Overlapping of forms. I'm also working on a long poem which looks like it might become a self-portrait in verse. I'm writing on very traditional subjects again and poems that rhyme occasionally. I'm writing a poem to Keats and a poem to Colette and a poem to the moon and a poem to Spring. After all the wild stuff in my first two books, here I am writing poems to Keats and to Spring.*

NYQ: You've spoken about the frustration of writing from the point of view of a woman. Did you get to the point where you felt trapped by your subject matter?

EJ: It took me a long time to break through to the freedom of writing out of a woman's voice, and then it seemed to be *all* I was writing about. Now I want to go beyond that. Sexuality is an important part of life, and sometimes it seems to be *all* of life. But there are other subjects. One tends to become impatient with oneself and doesn't want to repeat the things one has learned.

NYQ: That doesn't mean you won't come back to it.

EJ: I don't know. I don't have any program. I just sit down and write. When I have enough poems, I'll see if they make a book. I didn't realize that *Half-Lives* was a book which dealt with unfulfillment and emptiness until I began putting the poems together. Then it became apparent to me that I had subterranean rivers of imagery in those poems. Certain themes repeated

*These poems appear in *Loveroot* by Erica Jong (Holt, Rinehart and Winston, 1975).

24 /

themselves and I saw that a lot of the poems dealt with emptiness, wholeness, halfness, and so on. And a book began to come together. So I arranged the sections the way they naturally fell. I can't tell you what the third book* will be "about" until I see what poems accumulate. But I am quite sure that at certain periods in your life you deal with certain themes; and if you grow, those themes have to change.

NYQ: We wanted to ask you some questions about translation. Have any of your poems been translated into other languages? And then do you ever do translations? Do you read poetry in foreign languages?

EJ: I don't read poetry in foreign languages. Although I know some foreign languages tolerably in a kind of school way, and used to be able to speak some of them when I lived in the countries where they were spoken, I don't really know any language well enough to translate. I suppose I don't try translation because I write prose when I'm not writing poetry.

NYQ: When you speak of translations as the kind of thing poets can do, what recommendations would you make to a young poet about choosing something in a related field like translations or teaching or something entirely different to be a way of surviving economically while he struggles?

EJ: I think the best thing for a young poet is to grow up in Latin America. And to be made a diplomat.

NYQ: Like a Neruda.

EJ: We don't have ways of rewarding our poets like that. I don't know what a poet can do to survive. Everything you think of has terrible disadvantages. If you're a college teacher, you're always up to your neck in bad student writing. If you're an editor you get so weary of books being thrust at you that the printed word almost loses its force. Advertising is not

*Loveroot.

the most joyous profession. (I know poets who do all these things.) Maybe the best "profession" for a poet is to be born very wealthy. When I was in graduate school, I was told to get my PhD in English and to use my summers to write. I found that getting a PhD in English was not conducive to writing at all.

NYQ: How do you feel about confessional poetry?

EJ: There is no such a *thing* as confessional poetry. Anne Sexton gets branded with that and it's absurd. I think it's become a putdown term for women, a sexist label for women's poetry. People who use the term are falling into the subject-matter fallacy. Subject matter doesn't make a poem. And so a critic who uses that term is showing his total ignorance of what poetry is about.

There is this tendency to think that if you could only find the magic way, then you could become a poet. "Tell me how to become a poet. Tell me what to do." Is there a given subject that makes you a poet? Well, that's ridiculous. What makes you a poet is a gift for language, an ability to see into the heart of things, and an ability to deal with important unconscious material. When all those things come together, you're a poet. But there isn't one little gimmick that makes you a poet. There isn't any formula for it.

NYQ: In general, modern poetry requires (underline one): more vegetables, fewer vegetables, all of the above, none of the above.

EJ: The answer is: All of the above.

NYQ: That gets into your whole minimal vs. maximal poetry. You want everything.

EJ: I do want to get everything into my poetry. I want to get the whole world in. Colette had a term for it. She said that she wanted the "impure." Life was impure and that was what she wanted in her art—all the junk and jumble of things. Wallace Stevens also uses the images of a man on a dump: the poet—the man sitting on the dump. Life is full of all kinds of wonderful crap. Splendid confusion. Poetry should be able to take it all in.

NYQ: What do you think of interviews?

EJ: You always read them and say, "Oh, no. That's not me." No matter how candid you are, you *hate* the person you seem to be. But I understand the impulse to get a person down on paper. And the interview is a profoundly contemporary form: a conversation set in type. Often though, I've read interviews with myself and have been appalled. Yes, I had said almost that and almost that and almost something like that. But the gestalt was wrong. The end product was not me at all. Instead there was this creature bearing my name and face who made all sorts of foolish remarks out of context—and whom I disagreed with utterly on nearly everything.

This horrified reaction to one's own image is not only common to the person who finds herself anatomized in the media, but also to the novelist who must always finish her book in despair: "There . . . I've done my best and it still isn't good enough. Life is richer and more complex; life puts art to shame."

NYQ: You made a statement a while ago about writing from your inner landscape. And yet you also talk about writing as a woman poet. At a point when women poets are having a renaissance, how do you see this relationship between writing from this inner landscape and writing as who you are quite apart from where you live and the time you live in? And also being alive in a moment where there are lots of forces—psychoanalysis, the women's movement, moving down to the end of the century, and that kind of thing.

EJ: What should I answer first? One question at a time . . .

Actually, I don't think those things conflict. If you're writing about your inner landscape, you're writing about that inner landscape as female. It's female first and then beyond that, it's human. The two things don't cancel each other out. It's just a question of how you get there. Of course you're affected by the movements of your time, but not in a direct way. Look—I was not living in the United States between 1966 and 1969—which was the explosion of the hippie subculture, the flower children, the student revolutionaries—and yet there were many people who on reading *Fruits & Vegetables* saw me as a sort of flower child of that generation. If you're a poet, you *do* have your navel plugged in to the zeitgeist, and you *are* tuned in to the currents of your time. And not in a literal, obvious way. But your antennae are working. You don't plan it.

NYQ: A completely different question that we didn't ask you is if there are any reference works on the craft of poetry. For students to read or that you particularly love yourself.

EJ: You know the books I've recommended for my poetry seminar. And some of the other books I find really indispensable are: *The Glass House*, Allan Seager's biography of Theodore Roethke; Rilke's *Letters to a Young Poet*; Keats' letters; Mandelstam's *Hope Against Hope* (which shows you what it's like for a poet in a totalitarian country); books on mythology like *The Golden Bough* or *Women's Mysteries* or *The Great Mother*. I would certainly recommend *The Book of the It*, a book that really loosens up the imagination. I would very much recommend Theodore Roethke's *Straw for the Fire*, Virginia Woolf's *Writer's Notebook*, Colette's *Earthly Paradise*. Those are not books strictly speaking on the craft of writing, but I don't think you're going to learn much about poetry from reading about iambic pentameter, spondees, trochees and things like that. If that's what you're thinking of—a handbook. There are many good handbooks of poetry and I can't see that it would hurt you to read them. But for the most part you learn to be a poet (as Rilke says) by going into yourself and by reading lots of other writers. I think I once told you that when I began writing free verse, I read and re-read Denise Levertov's books. I figured that *she* knew where to break a line. Her white spaces on the page *meant* something. So I reread and reread her books, trying to figure out where she broke her lines and why. I might have gone to William Carlos Williams, too, because that was where she learned. You learn to write by reading the poets you love over and over and trying to figure out what they're doing and why they're doing it. You read Galway Kinnell's *Book of the Nightmares* and you see the way he interweaves certain images throughout the book. Study the poets you love. Read them again and again. That's how you learn to be a poet. Unfortunately though, talent is something you're born with. And that's not very democratic. A gift for language is essential. So is a feeling for the rhythms of prose and poetry. The other gift is stamina—the willingness to *do* it and *do* it and *do* it. I don't know where you get that. I knew plenty of people in college who had lots of talent, but never became writers. They gave up. A good portion of the struggle is just that willingness to keep on doing it. Ultimately, I would say I write because it gives me a great deal of pleasure to write. I would rather write than do almost anything else. Somebody will say to me: "Oh, you've been very productive," and the implication is that I've been disciplined and plodding. But writing is such an incredible joy and pleasure that at times it scarcely feels like work. There are also bad times, though.

NYQ: Have you ever thought of another career?

EJ: I thought of being a painter and for years I did paint. There was a time when I wanted very much to be a doctor. At one time I thought I was going to be a college professor. And, of course, I still teach on a part-time basis. But I think writing is the only profession which has enough surprises in store to hold me for the rest of my life. If you keep growing and changing, writing is an endless voyage of discovery. The surprises never stop. All that runs out is time.

FRUITS & VEGETABLES

For Jonathan & Alice,
who know the poems
inside the fruits & vegetables

Contents

THE OBJECTIVE WOMAN

FLOWER EATERS

"Poetry, the creative act, the archetypal
sexual act. Sexuality is poetry. . . .
Petrarch says that he invented the beautiful
name of Laura, but that in reality Laura
was nothing but the poetic laurel which
he had pursued with incessant labor."

* * *

"We must eat again of the tree of knowledge
in order to fall into innocence."

NORMAN O. BROWN

FRUITS & VEGETABLES

"It is hard to imagine a civilization
without onions."

JULIA CHILD

"Only weggebobbles and fruit. . .
I wouldn't be surprised if it was
that kind of food you see produces
the like waves of the brain the
poetical."

JAMES JOYCE

"In recent decades there has been a
distinct falling off in the interest
shown in hunger artists."

FRANZ KAFKA

"Know me come eat with me."
JAMES JOYCE

1

Goodbye, he waved, entering the apple.
That red siren,
whose white flesh turns brown
with prolonged exposure to air,
opened her perfect cheeks to receive him.
She took him in.
The garden revolved
in her glossy patinas of skin.
Goodbye.

2

O note the two round holes in onion.

3

Did I tell you about
my mother's avocado?
She grew it from a pit.
Secretly, slowly in the dark,
it put out grub-white roots
which filled a jelly jar.
From this unlikely start,
an avocado tree with bark
& dark green leaves
shaded the green silk couch
which shaded me

throughout my shady adolescence.
There, beneath that tree
my skirt gave birth to hands!
Oh memorable hands of boys
with blacked-out eyes
like culprits
in the *National Enquirer*.
My mother nursed that tree
like all her children,
turned it around so often
towards the sun
that its trunk grew twisted
as an old riverbed,
& despite its gaudy leaves
it never bore
fruit.

4

Cantaloupes: the setting sun at Paestum
slashed by rosy columns.

5

I am thinking of the onion again, with its two O mouths,
like the gaping holes in nobody. Of the outer skin, pinkish
brown, peeled to reveal a greenish sphere, bald as a dead
planet, glib as glass, & an odor almost animal. I consider
its ability to draw tears, its capacity for self-scrutiny,
flaying itself away, layer on layer, in search of its heart
which is simply another region of skin, but deeper &

greener. I remember Peer Gynt; I consider its sometimes
double heart. Then I think of despair when the onion
searches its soul & finds only its various skins; & I think
of the dried tuft of roots leading nowhere & the parched
umbilicus, lopped off in the garden. Not self-righteous
like the proletarian potato, nor a siren like the apple. No
show-off like the banana. But a modest, self-effacing vegetable, questioning, introspective, peeling itself away, or
merely radiating halos like lake ripples. I consider it the
eternal outsider, the middle child, the sad analysand of
the vegetable kingdom. Glorified only in France (otherwise silent sustainer of soups & stews), unloved for itself
alone—no wonder it draws our tears! Then I think again
how the outer peel resembles paper, how soul & skin
merge into one, how each peeling strips bare a heart
which in turn turns skin. . .

6

A poet in a world without onions,
in a world without apples
regards the earth as a great fruit.

Far off, galaxies glitter like currants.
The whole edible universe drops
to his watering mouth. . .

Think of generations of mystics
salivating for the fruit of god,
of poets yearning to inhabit apples,
of the sea, that dark fruit,
closing much more quickly than a wound,
of the nameless galaxies of astronomers,
hoping that the cosmos will ripen
& their eyes will become tongues. . .

7

For the taste of the fruit
is the tongue's dream,
& the apple's red
is the passion of the eye.

8

If a woman wants to be a poet,
she must dwell in the house of the tomato.

9

It is not an emptiness,
the fruit between your legs,
but the long hall of history,
& dreams are coming down the hall
by moonlight.

10

They push up through the loam
like lips of mushrooms.

11

(Artichoke, after Child): Holding the heart base up, rotate it slowly with your left hand against the blade of a knife held firmly in your right hand to remove all pieces of ambition & expose the pale surface of the heart. Frequently rub the cut portions with gall. Drop each heart as it is finished into acidulated water. The choke can be removed after cooking.

12

(Artichoke, after Neruda)

It is green at the artichoke heart,
but remember the times
you flayed
leaf after leaf,
hoarding the pale silver paste
behind the fortresses of your teeth,
tonguing the vinaigrette,
only to find the husk of a worm
at the artichoke heart?
The palate reels like a wronged lover.
Was all that sweetness counterfeit?
Must you vomit back
world after vegetable world
for the sake of one worm
in the green garden of the heart?

13

But the poem about bananas has not yet been written. Southerners worry a lot about bananas. Their skin. And nearly everyone worries about the size of bananas, as if that had anything to do with flavor. Small bananas are sometimes quite sweet. But bananas are like poets: they only want to be told how great they are. Green bananas want to be told they're ripe. According to Freud, girls envy bananas. In America chocolate syrup & whipped cream have been known to enhance the flavor of bananas. This is called a *banana split*.

14

The rice is pregnant.
It swells past its old transparency.
Hard, translucent worlds inside the grains
open like fans. It is raining rice!
The peasants stand under oiled
rice paper umbrellas cheering.

Someone is scattering rice from the sky!
Chopper blades mash the clouds.
The sky browns like cheese soufflé.
Rice grains puff & pop open.

"What have we done to deserve this?"
the peasants cry. Even the babies
are cheering. Cheers slide from their lips
like spittle. Old men kick their clogs
into the air & run in the rice paddies
barefoot. This is a monsoon! A wedding!

Each grain has a tiny invisible parachute.
Each grain is a rain drop.

"They have sent us rice!" the mothers scream,
opening their throats to the smoke. . .

15

Here should be a picture of my favorite apple.
It is also a nude & bottle.
It is also a landscape.
There are no such things as still lives.

16

In general, modern poetry requires (underline one):
a) more fruit; b) less fruit; c) more vegetables; d) less
vegetables; e) all of the above; f) none of the above.

17

Astonishment of apples. Every fall.
But only Italians are into grapes,
calling them eggs.
O my eggs,
branching off my family tree,
my father used to pluck you,
leaving bare twigs on the dining room table,
leaving mother furious on the dining room table:

picked clean.
Bare ruined choirs
where late the sweet.
A pile of pits.

18

Adam naming the fruit
after the creation of fruit,
his tongue tickling
the crimson lips of the pomegranate,
the tip of his penis licking
the cheeks of the peach,
quince petals in his hair,
his blue arms full of plums,
his legs wrapped around watermelons,
dandling pumpkins on his fatherly knees,
tomatoes heaped around him in red pyramids. . .

peach
peach
peach
peach
peach

he sighs

to kingdom come.

TOUCH

"*The spirit moves, but not always upward.*"

THEODORE ROETHKE

Seven

The 7 mysterious holes in the body
:
                        the sacredness of 7
                        depends on these

The 5 holes in the head
:
                        the Moloch of the mouth
                        & gluttony the 5th of deadly sins
                        the ears O stop them
                        the 2 roads of the nostrils
                        leading to Rome

But the eyes are not holes
; they are scars
remains of a time
when the whole body was eye
& light flowed everywhere
like sperm

                        The 7 mysterious holes
                        do not include
                        :
                        the navel,
                        that link
                        with a vegetable
                        world,
                        that green vine
                        rooting toward
                        earth

;
but the anus loves
poetry
& is prolific

       & the hole in the penis
       sings to the cunt

              :

              of the pyramids of Egypt
              & the hanging gardens of
              Babylon
              & the 7th day of Creation

There is, for example, the 7th heaven of the Mohammedans
& the 7th circle of hell, moated with blood

There is Dante climbing down the caves of flesh
There are the 7 hills
the 7 seas

With Silk

A girl with silk pockets
& eyes slipperier than fish
was waiting if she ever let him go—
her Chinese lover
with balls
like fresh lichees
& tongue on her tongue
like a kumquat.
At night
he entered the body
of her dream,
his black hair
massed on his forehead,
his tennis trophies ranged
in barriers around them,
his long legs leaping
towards love
or some ground stroke.
His body was white
in the dream light,
his penis dark
as a tree.
She would never know
who the other was,
waiting,
speaking her high-pitched Mandarin
like wind chimes,
trilling syllables
he never understood,
binding & unbinding her feet
as if they were hearts.
She sits
on a grass mat
scented with jasmine,
her hands mannered
as an old scroll painting,
her eyes fishing.
They hook on his
while he makes love to her.
A syllable of moonlight
shatters
on the floor.

The Sheets

We used to meet
on this corner
in the same wind.
It fought us up the hill
to your house,
blew us in the door.
The elevator rose
on gusts of stale air
fed on ancient dinners.
Your room smelled
of roach spray and roses.

In those days
we went to bed with Marvell.
The wind ruffled sheets and pages,
spoke to us through walls.
For hours I used to lie
with my ear to your bare chest,
listening for the sea.

Now the wind is tearing
the building down.
The sheets are rising.

They billow through the air like sails.

White with your semen,
holding invisible prints
of the people we were,
the people we might have been,
they sail across the country
disguised as clouds.

Momentarily they snag
on the Rocky Mountains,
then rise
shredded into streamers.

Now they are bannering westward
over California
where your existence
is rumored.

The Quarrel

It is a rainy night
when the wind beats at your door
like a man you have turned away

He comes back trailing leaves & branches
He comes back in a shower of earth
He comes back with blades of grass
still clinging to his hair

No matter how hard he holds you
he is still elsewhere
making love to another

No matter how hard you hold him
you are still
elsewhere

Your bodies slide together
like wet grass blades
You cling & stop the raindrops
with your tongues

Later you rise
& pick the nettles from your hair
You take the leaves for clothing

Your loneliness
is a small gray hole in the rain
You rise & go knocking
at his locked front door

Downward

Because your eyes are the color of shadows on Chartres
Cathedral
  because your sunglasses are smoke
   because smoke curls out of your ears to music
    because your mustache shades the letters of your words
    because your neck is planted in your shoulders
     because your tiny nipples rise to meet my tongue
      because the navel of your earth has never been
discovered by Columbus
    because we are going downward

     Because the black hair whorls on your belly
    because your knees are mountain ranges
     because my mouth is a valley of melting snow
    because your penis is no metaphor
    because your thighs are horses galloping
     because your feet are the beginning & the
beginning again
     because their soles tattoo the air
      because we are going we are going
downward

Touch

A man in armor,
a huge plume
shooting from his head,
velvet buckles at his hips,
joints of oiled steel
moving with the sound
of taffeta,
comes to my room
late at night.

His face is visored.
His chest
is emblazoned with crowns.
A fine tattoo of gold
blooms on his arms.

Through a chink in the visor
I see what may be an eye,
or perhaps the reflection
of its loss.

His codpiece gleams like a knife.

I think myself naked,
my skin white
as the cut side of a pear.
I think he will slash me.

But when we move
our bodies together
we make such noises. . .

It has been this way for years.
Our steel hands clasp.
Our legs lock into place
like coupling freight trains.

His Silence

He still wears the glass skin of childhood.
Under his hands, the stones turn mirrors.
His eyes are knives.

Who froze the ground to his feet?
Who locked his mouth into an horizon?
Why does the sun set when we touch?

I look for the lines between the silences.
He looks only for the silences.

Cram this page under his tongue.
Open him as if for surgery.
Let the red knife love slide in.

The Ecological Apocalypse
as Foretold to Adam & Eve

Because he dreams of seeding the world with words
his eyes bite
She looks   He looks away
He is snowblind
from staring at her breasts
They make love
This is marked by asterisks
those gaps
disguised as stars

      *   *   *

He thinks the future is a mouth
She invites him
into her apple

The Man Under the Bed

The man under the bed
The man who has been there for years waiting
The man who waits for my floating bare foot
The man who is silent as dustballs riding the darkness
The man whose breath is the breathing of small white
                                        butterflies
The man whose breathing I hear when I pick up the
                                        phone
The man in the mirror whose breath blackens silver
The boneman in closets who rattles the mothballs
The man at the end of the end of the line

I met him tonight   I always meet him
He stands in the amber air of a bar
When the shrimp curl like beckoning fingers
& ride through the air on their toothpick skewers
When the ice cracks & I am about to fall through
he arranges his face around its hollows
he opens his pupilless eyes at me
For years he has waited to drag me down
& now he tells me
he has only waited to take me home
We waltz through the street like death & the maiden
We float through the wall of the wall of my room

If he's my dream he will fold back into my body
His breath writes letters of mist on the glass of my cheeks
I wrap myself around him like the darkness
I breathe into his mouth
& make him real

HERE COMES

"*What is anti-poetry?*

* * *

A woman with her legs open?

* * *

A jet-propelled coffin?"

NICANOR PARRA

Arse Poetica

for Leonard Robinson & Patricia Goedicke

I

Item: the poet has to feed herself & fuck herself.

II

Salt the metaphors. Set them breast up over the vegetables
& baste them with the juice in the casserole. Lay a piece
of aluminum foil over the poem, cover the casserole &
heat it on top of the stove until you hear the images
sizzling. Then place the poem in the middle of a rack in
the preheated oven.

Roast for an hour & twenty minutes, regulating heat so
that poem is always making quiet cooking noises. The
poem is done when drumsticks move in their sockets &
the last drops of juice drained from the vent run clear.
Remove to a serving dish & discard trussing.

III

Once the penis has been introduced into the poem, the
poet lets herself down until she is sitting on the muse
with her legs outside him. He need not make any motions
at all. The poet sits upright & raises & lowers her body
rhythmically until the last line is attained. She may pause
in her movements & may also move her pelvis & abdomen
forward & back or sideways, or with a circular corkscrew
motion. This method yields exceptionally acute images
& is, indeed, often recommended as yielding the summit

of aesthetic enjoyment. Penetration is at its deepest. Conception, however, is less apt than with other attitudes.

This position is also suitable when the muse is tired or lacking in vigor since the poet plays the active role. Penetration is deepest when the poet's body makes an angle of 45 degrees with the muse's. A half-erect muse will remain in position when this attitude is adopted since he cannot slip out of the poem.

The Teacher

The teacher stands before the class.
She's talking of Chaucer.
But the students aren't hungry for Chaucer.
They want to devour her.
They are eating her knees, her toes, her breasts, her eyes
& spitting out
her words.
What do they want with words?
They want a real lesson!

She is naked before them.
Psalms are written on her thighs.
When she walks, sonnets divide
into octaves & sestets.
Couplets fall into place
when her fingers nervously toy
with the chalk.

But the words don't clothe her.
No amount of poetry can save her now.
There's no volume big enough to hide in.
No unabridged Webster, no OED.

The students aren't dumb.
They want a lesson.
Once they might have taken life
by the scruff of its neck
in a neat couplet.
But now
they need blood.

They have left Chaucer alone
& have eaten the teacher.

She's gone now.
Nothing remains
but a page of print.
She's past our helping.
Perhaps she's part of her students.
(Don't ask how.)

Eat this poem.

Walking Through the Upper East Side

All over the district, on leather couches
& brocade couches, on daybeds
& "professional divans," they are confessing.
The air is thick with it,
the ears of the analysts must be sticky.

Words fill the air above couches & hover there
hanging like smog. I imagine
impossible Steinberg scrolls,
unutterable sounds suspended in inked curlicues
while the Braque print & the innocuous Utrillo
look on look on look on.

My six analysts, for example—

the sly Czech who tucked his shoelaces
under the tongues of his shoes,
the mistress of social work with orange hair,
the famous old German who said:
"You sink, zerefore you are,"
the bouncy American who loved to talk dirty,
the bitchy widow of a famous theoretician,
& another—or was it two?—I have forgotten—
they rise like a Greek chorus in my dreams.
They reproach me for my messy life.
They do not offer to refund my money.

& the others—siblings for an hour or so—
ghosts whom I brushed in & out of the door.
Sometimes the couch was warm from their bodies.
Only our coats knew each other,
rubbing shoulders in the dark closet.

Digging the Chinese Cemetery

(near the grave of my grandfather-in-law)

The Chinese Christian Burial Association
has grouped politely on the shores
of the new world.

The members softly call the roll
so as not to wake
the sleepwalkers.

America is here beneath these elms.
The Chinese Christian Burial Association
is about to enter it.

Pon Fung Chen Lee Moy
Wong Tong Tsien Tsang Chew
Chang Chan Jong Long Song. . . .

The Chinese Christian Burial Association
is digging
home.

Here Comes

(a flip through Bride's)

The silver spoons
were warbling
their absurd musical names
when, drawing back
her veil (illusion),

she stepped into
the valentine-shaped bathtub,
& slid her perfect bubbles
in between
the perfect bubbles.

Oh brilliantly complex as
compound interest,
her diamond gleams
(Forever) on the edge
of a weddingcake-shaped bed.

What happens there
is merely icing since
a snakepit of dismembered
douchebag coils (all writhing)
awaits her on the tackier back pages.

Dearly beloved, let's hymn
her (& Daddy) down
the aisle with
epithalamions composed
for Ovulen ads:

"It's the right
of every (married) couple
to wait   to space   to wait"
—& antistrophes
appended by the Pope.

Good Grief—the groom!
Has she (or we)
entirely forgot?
She'll dream him whole.
American type with ushers

halfbacks headaches drawbacks backaches
& borrowed suit
stuffed in a borrowed face
(or was it the reverse?)
Oh well. Here's he:

part coy pajamas,
part mothered underwear
& of course
an enormous prick
full of money.

Fracture

This constant ache
is my leg's message to me.
"Hello. Hello. Hello.
You're getting there," it says,
"step by step."

Legs aren't stars
which sputter out
& go on gleaming anyway.
I've lived, of course,
with phantom limbs

but this fracture
doesn't point to
amputation. No.
It hisses something
much more final.

Skin lantern,
necklace of teeth,
the bones & sinews
are in revolt against us.
We keep them down

with little bribes:
vitamins, penicillin,
& now these pounds of plaster,
but they will bury us,
good bolsheviks,

& know it.
So they've got time to bide.

Meanwhile: spread-eagled
on these crutches, a cripple
sucking the ground with rubber

nipples, or else a knight,
up to my ass in armor,
I limp & swing my way
across the street
& up the steps,

moving, here & now,
step by step,
towards the future,
that incurable
fracture.

Two More Scenes from the Lives of the Vegetables

> "(*only the knife knows the heart of the yam*)"
> E.N. SARGENT

I: Borscht

We entered Russia backwards through the borscht,
paddling our kayak of sour cream,
legs hanging down in the crimson water,
& the banks resounding
with Russian Tea Room Music,
movie scores from *Docteur Z.*

It was a miserable winter in Paris,
all the girls at Le Drugstore wearing Zhivago coats,
& the Hotel Stella turning off the heat
& only cold water in the bidets.

But here in the soup it's cozy.
Your cheeks are ruddy from reflections on the water.
Birches bend over the bowl of the lake.
Chekhov rides up to meet us in a one-horse shay.
Somewhere I think I see a black monk come floating. . .

The waiters all look like Tolstoy's peasants—
except they speak Yiddish.
One gave a violin recital once in Town Hall.

The soup is substantial.
You could almost walk on it as if it were water.
It is biblical, in fact: a red sea.
Look! Someone has written "Yuri loves Lara" in sour
                                                    cream!

II: Carrot

They dangle the carrot before our eyes.
We walk.
It bounces against the green sky.
Its leaves droop, a wounded parachute.
We have always walked behind it.
Actually we believe the carrot to be
God's penis.
That is why we walk behind it.
It is disappointing, wrinkled and small.
It's the only one we've got.
How we dream of a great carrot to follow!
Blown up like a Macy's balloon on Thanksgiving,
floating over the prismatic static of color T.V.,
it seems to point the way
with a finger so large no one can doubt it.
But our carrot is more dead than alive.
Flies fly in halo formation around it.
Worms peek out, waving goodbye.
Even the dirt will not cling to it.
The root hairs hang down
like the skimpy beards of ancient Chinamen.
We continue to walk behind it.
Someday, they will stop the cart
and let us eat it.
By then it will be cleft with a black valley.
It will hold landscapes, a whole geography of fear.
And by then too, our teeth will have fallen out.
They will strew the road behind us,
breadcrumbs for Hansel & Gretel.

Cheese

Spelunking through the blue caves of the Roquefort
under a golden Gouda moon,
we thought of the breasts of the Virgin
which are also blue. Very few
cheeses are,
and Mary does not belong
in a poem on cheese.
                        Or does She?
We are mice in this wedge
of cheesy poetry, we are about
to be trapped.
                        How peaceful (on the other hand) to be a
                                                        cheese!

To merge with the Great Eater
as every mystic (or mouse)
has some time wished.

Goudas whirl in the sky,
shedding their rinds like prayer wheels;
already the Brie is soft with ecstasy.
Look for that Bel Paese which saints speak of
where the holes dream the Swiss cheese,
where plate and knife exist only in visions,
where milk and cream
are merely memories,
like history,
like Mary.

THE OBJECTIVE WOMAN

*Woman's a long moan of a word
with a man in it...*

The Commandments

*"You don't really want to be a poet. First
of all, if you're a woman, you have to be
three times as good as any of the men.
Secondly, you have to fuck everyone. And
thirdly, you have to be dead."*
　　　　　A MALE POET, IN CONVERSATION

If a woman wants to be a poet,
　she should sleep near the moon with her face open;
　she should walk through herself studying the landscape;
　she should not write her poems in menstrual blood.

If a woman wants to be a poet,
　she should run backwards circling the volcano;
　she should feel for the movement along her faults;
　she should not get a Ph.D. in seismography.

If a woman wants to be a poet,
　she should not sleep with uncircumcised manuscripts;
　she should not write odes to her abortions;
　she should not make stew of old unicorn meat.

If a woman wants to be a poet,
　she should read French cookbooks and Chinese
　　　　　　　　　　　　　　　　vegetables,
　she should suck on French poets to freshen her breath;
　she should not masturbate in writing seminars.

If a woman wants to be a poet,
　she should peel back the hair from her eyeballs;
　she should listen to the breathing of sleeping men;
　she should listen to the spaces between that breathing.

If a woman wants to be a poet,
   she should not write her poems with a dildo;
   she should pray that her daughters are women;
   she should forgive her father for his bravest sperm.

Aging

(balm for a 27th birthday)

Hooked for two years now on wrinkle creams   creams for
crowsfeet   ugly lines (if only there were one!)
any perfumed grease   which promises   youth   beauty
not truth   but all I need on earth
      I've been studying   how women age

                                    how

it starts around the eyes   so you can tell
a woman of 22 from one of 28 merely by
a faint scribbling near the lids   a subtle crinkle
      a fine line
extending from the fields of vision

                                    this

in itself is not unbeautiful   promising
      as it often does
insights which clear-eyed 22 has no inkling of
promising   certain sure-thighed things in bed
certain fingers on your spine & lids

                                    but

it's only the beginning   as ruin proceeds downward
lingering for a while around the mouth   hardening the smile
into prearranged patterns (irreversible!)   writing furrows
from the wings of the nose   (oh nothing much at first
      but "showing promise"   like your early poems

                                    of deepening)

& plotting lower to the corners of the mouth   drooping them
a little   like the tragic mask   though not at all grotesque
as yet   & then as you sidestep   into the 4th decade
beginning to crease the neck   (just slightly)
   though the breasts below

                                            especially

when they're small (like mine) may stay high far
      into the thirties
still the neck will give you away   & after that the chin
which   though you may snip it back & hike it up under
your earlobes will never quite love your bones as it once did

                                            though

the belly may be kept firm through numerous pregnancies
by means of sit-ups jogging dancing (think of Russian ballerinas)
      & the cunt
as far as I know is ageless   possibly immortal   becoming simply
more open   more quick to understand   more dry-eyed than at 22

                                            which

after all   is what you were dying for   (as you ravaged
islands of turtles beehives oysterbeds the udders of cows)
desperate to censor changes which you simply might have let play
over you lying back listening opening yourself
      letting the years make love the only way   (poor blunderers)

                                            they know

Bitter Pills for the Dark Ladies

*"—hardly a person at all, or a woman,
certainly not another 'poetess,' but. . ."*
ROBERT LOWELL ABOUT SYLVIA PLATH

If you've got to   if after trying to
give it up (like smoking or Nembutal)
if after swearing to   shut it up   it keeps on
yakking (that voice in your head)
that insomniac who lives across the wall,
that amateur Hammondist
who plays those broken scales next door
o then   consider yourself doomed to.

Ambition bites. Bite back.
(It's almost useless.) Suppose yourself born
half black, half Jewish in Missis-
sippi, & with one leg
                        You get the Idear?
Jus' remember you got no rights. Anything go wrong
they gonna roun' you up & howl "Poetess!"
(sorta like "Nigra!") then kick the shit outa you
sayin': You got Natural Rhythm (28 days)
so why you wanna mess aroun'?

Words bein' slippery & poetry bein'
mos'ly a matter of balls,
men what gives in to the lilt and lift of words
(o love   o death   o organ tones   o dickey!)
is "Cosmic." You is "Sentimental."
So dance in your Master's bed (or thesis) & shut
yo' mouth. Ain't you happiest there?

If they let you out   it's as Supermansaint
played by S. Poitier   with Ph.D.[2]   & a buttondown fly
washed whiter than any other on the block.
& the ultimate praise is always a question of nots:
                              viz. not like a woman
                              viz. "certainly not another 'poetess' "

meanin'

            she got a cunt but she don't talk funny
            & he's a nigger but he don't smell funny

& the only good poetess is a dead.

The Objective Woman

I

For I praise the women of America with their electric
                    purple sunglasses
          & disposable nipples
For I praise their cherryfrost lips & the ivory blizzards
          of their fingernails
For I praise the firmness of their ultralucence
          & the ultralucence of their firmessence
For I praise their nail & moondrops, their cupid's quiver
                    douches
For I praise their eyewriters & what is written on their
                    eyes
For I praise their bodysmooth clingthings, their curvalon
                    braslips
For I praise their odor of bluegrass, their elusive tigress
                    white shoulders
For I praise their candied brandy toenails which grow
                    longer after death
For I praise their deodorized armpits & their sprayed
          & powdered crotches
For & praise their electric typewriters which never stop
                    humming
          & the hearts of their men which stop
For I praise their vacuum cleaners which howl with their
                    own voiceless rage
For I praise their electronic answering machines, their
                    plug-in mothers
For I praise young women twisting their wedding bands
          & old women with empty wombs & full
                    shopping bags
For I praise crones with rouged wrinkles who shop
          in garbage

For I praise all women awaiting repairmen
                        & all women who sleep with bottles
For I praise shopping carts & stirrups
                        & ten-cent rest rooms
For I praise women who buy shoes which hurt
                        & hats which are unreturnable
For I praise their outsides which become their insides
          & their insides which shall become their outsides

II

The Nose

The evidence mounts.
The bottles line up backward
in her mirror.
In each golden hollow floats
an embalmed homunculus.
Ambush.
Enormous dirigible roses
are blooming
in the corners of the room.
They float up
& explode against the ceiling.
Someone is planting orange trees in Versailles
& tending vats of perfume.
There's a tiger yawning in the four-poster
(reading "The Story of O").
On the night table: Tabu, Russian Leather, Vol de Nuit.
"What makes a shy girl get Intimate?"
"There is only one Joy."
& suddenly the gilded cupids
make obscene gestures.
She thinks,

"She looked deep into herself & found nothing."
The mad-eyed violinist is about to seize
the lady pianist.
"Tigress," he growls, "Iced Tigress."
"Toujours Moi," she replies.
The country of the nose.

III

The Rings

After her husband died,
she had his wedding band
soldered to her own.
He was buried bare-handed,
slid into the earth.
Her hands move among the objects
which pretend to be my life.
She wears both rings on one finger.

Was it gold she sought to spare?
Or was she scared
of being married to a dead man?
How were their fingers linked?
Their mouths?
He was buried with his gold teeth on.
Darling, till death do us.

IV

The Dryer

Cleaned & peeled & sealed
down to her fingertips,
unabel to touch
or smell herself,
her capsule stuffed
with thumbed copies
of "Vogue" & "Bazaar,"
her urine siphoned off
into the classified files
of the CIA,
her hair standing
weightlessly on end,
wind whipping
around her helmeted ears,
the first female American astronaut
is being launched!
She rises like Beatrice
into a sky
where all the stars
are Florentine gold.

No love is made
by touch in paradise.
Only the minds meeting
in concentric rings
of wind & bells,
only the legs of the compasses
meshing & turning.
Solitary mute,

always awaiting
the prince for whom
it will be worthwhile
to shake the meteors
out of her hair.
He comes.
He combs her out.
He's gay.

V

OB-GYN

Probing the long poem of her body
where she lies riding,
her knees framing his face,
her breasts & belly tented white,
he looks away
as if forgetting
that his hand
has disappeared.

It's dark.

He chatters about ski resorts.

Does she prefer Kitzbühel to Aspen?

He's touched some tiny town
high in the alps
where the sky sinks its blue teeth
into the mountains
& the sun slides down behind the peaks
like buttered rum.

A light goes on
in the uppermost chalet
above the tree line.
(Your ovaries are fine.)

Bring light!
A miner's hat or flashlight.
Is it like climbing Everest at night?
One false step empties you back into the sky?
What do the eyes of the fingertips hook on?
Skeletons from lost expeditions?
Babies with the faces of old men?
The womb blooming, a forest of peonies?

Not applicable.
Your poems are codes.
Pap. BI. CA.
Uptake. Follow-up.

You look away.

You tell me how expert you are.

I see that you stay upright
on the surface of the snow.

But I imagine how
the dark core of the mountain
sucks at your dreams
& I see you threading
a black forest
taking the curves gently
knowing it doesn't matter
if you ski through trees
easily looping left & right

Or falling
as if falling asleep
the shudder of your teeth
the spasm of your falling into her
moving through trees at night
moving through branches

Skiers above you
charms on a long bracelet
blue-faced angels
angels in animal fur

trusting the edge
you leave
no footprints

FLOWER EATERS

"*The shadow is bluest when the body
that casts it has vanished.*"

RAFAEL ALBERTI

The Man Giving Birth in the Dark

The man giving birth in the dark
has died
& come back
to life again,

is stretching out his arms
in the dark
as if to embrace
favorite ghosts.

His heart stops
& starts.
Once more
he has been pardoned

for nothing.
It is my father
making the darkness
into daughters.

Living In

(*my grandmother's house*)

We entered you like a house,
blowing along
the white curtains.

In the kitchen
with its old aroma of pot roast,
in among the cannisters of tea,
the lavendered closets
with pillowed rows of pink soap,
boxes of cottonwool
& unfinished embroideries,

we said
how we'd like to be lived in
after our death.

Then we began to replace you,
seeping in like cave water,
changing your old order,
defending ourselves
with our own smells.

(I poured espresso
from your teapot,
hung black curtains
in your bathroom.)

Sometimes,
coming home suddenly,
I'd catch you,
your cheek as soft as willow tips,

shaking your head from side to side,
denying
the cancer that was eating you.

I knew
your ghost as my own wish
& wasn't frightened,
but you
refused to stay.

Now, armored by our walls of books,
paintings you wouldn't have approved
& foods you'd never taste,
we find ourselves
alone at last.

Yesterday
we visited your grave.

You were all there.

In Sylvia Plath Country

for Grace Darling Griffin

The skin of the sea
has nothing to tell me.

I see her diving down
into herself—

past the bell-shaped jellyfish
who toll for no one—

& meaning to come back.

＊

In London, in the damp
of a London morning,
I see her sitting,
folding & unfolding herself,
while the blood
hammers like rain
on her heart's windows.

This is her own country—
the sea, the rain
& death half rhyming
with her father's name.

Obscene monosyllable,
it lingers for a while
on the roof
of the mouth's house.

I stand here
savoring the sound,
like salt.

*

They thought your death
was your last poem:
a black book
with gold-tooled cover
& pages the color of ash.

But I thought different,
knowing how madness
doesn't believe
in metaphor.

When you began to feel
the drift of continents
beneath your feet,
the sea's suck,
& each
atom of the poisoned air,
you lost
the luxury of simile.

Gull calls, broken shells,
the quarried coast.
This is where America ends,
dropping off
to the depths.

Death comes
differently in California.
Marilyn stalled
in celluloid,
the frame stuck,

& the light
burning through.

Bronze to her platinum,
Ondine, Ariel,
finally no one,

what could we tell you
after you dove down into yourself
& were swallowed
by your poems?

A Reading

The old poet
with his face full of lines,
with iambs jumping in his hair like fleas,
with all the revisions of his body
unsaying him,
walks to the podium.

He is about to tell us
how he came to this.

Imaginary Landscapes

for my parents

Who are these small determined figures
            with turbaned heads
                        coming
to doric temples
                        in
                                    fifteenth-century galleons
                with
medieval castles
                in the background?
            They speak
                        & gesture in the halflight,
                                    bring
                cattle, parcels
                                    to the classic shore
            below the gothic hill.
                        Sunlight moonlight twilight starlight
gleams across
            a stagey sea.
                                    Clouds toss. Sails fill.
            Windlessly,
                        what banners wave?
            Whose landscape
                                    is this mind?
Whose bluish breasts became
            these castled hills?
                                    Whose darkness is

this winter afternoon?
Whose darkness is
this darkening gallery?
Turn softly mind, wind,
Claude Lorrain,
Turner's making
light of Venice,
showing
his true
colors.

The Saturday Market

for Alexander Mitscherlich

Lumbering down
in the early morning clatter
from farms
where the earth was hard all winter,
the market women bear
grapes blue as the veins
of fair-skinned women,
cherries dark as blood,
roses strewn like carnage
on makeshift altars.
They come
in ancient rattling trucks
which sprout geraniums,
are stained
with strawberries.
Their fingers thick
& thorn-pricked,
their huge smock-pockets
jingling pennies,
they walk,
heavy goddesses,
while the market
blossoms into bleeding
all around them.
Currants which glitter
like Christmas ornaments
are staining
their wooden boxes.
Cherries, grapes—
everything
seems to be bleeding!
I think

how a sentimental
German poet
might have written
that the cut rose
mourns the garden
& the grapes
their Rhineland vineyard
(where the crooked vines
stretch out their arms
like dancers)
for this
is a sentimental country
& Germans
are passionate gardeners
who view with humanity
the blights of roses,
the adversities of vineyards.
But I am not fooled.
This bleeding is, no doubt,
in the beholder's eye,
& if
to tend a garden
is to be civilized,
surely this country
of fat cabbages
& love-lavished geraniums
would please
an eighteenth-century
philosopher.
Two centuries, however,
buzz above my head
like hornets over fruit.
I stuff my mouth with cherries
as I watch
the thorn-pricked fingers
of the market women
lifting & weighing,
weighing, weighing.

The Heidelberg Landlady

Because she lost her father
in the First World War,
her husband in the Second,
we don't dispute
"There's no Gemütlichkeit in America."

We're winning her heart
with filter cigarettes.
Puffing, she says,
"You can't judge a country
by just twelve years."

Gray days,
the wind hobbling down sidestreets,
I'm walking in a thirties photograph,
the prehistoric age
before my birth.

This town was never bombed.
Old ladies still wear funny shoes,
long, seedy furs.
They smell of camphor and camomile,
old photographs.

Nothing much happened here.
A few jewelry shops changed hands.
A brewery. Banks.
The university put up a swastika, took it down.
The students now chant HO CHI MINH & hate
                                        Americans

on principle.
Daddy wears a flyer's cap

& never grew old.
He's on the table with the teacakes.
Mother & grandma are widows.

They take care of things.
It rains nearly every day;
every day, they wash the windows.
They cultivate jungles in the front parlors,
lush tropics

framed by lacy white curtains.
They coax the earth with plant food, scrub the leaves.
Each plant shines like a fat child.
They hope for the sun,
living in a Jewless world without men.

Student Revolution

(Heidelberg, 1969)

After the teach-in
we smeared the walls with
our solidarity,
looked left, & saw
Marx among the angels,
singing the blues.

The students march,
I (spectator)
follow.
Here (as everywhere)
the Polizei
are clean, are clean.

In Frankfurt,
the whores lean out
their windows, screaming:
"Get a job—you dirty
hippies!" Or words
(auf Deutsch) to that effect.

I'm also waiting
for the Revolution,
friends.
Surely, my poems
will get better.
Surely, I'll no longer
fear my dreams.
Surely I won't murder
my capitalist father
each night
just to inherit
his love.

Flying You Home

> *"I only remember the onion, the egg and the boy.*
> *O that was me, said the madman."*
>
> NICHOLAS MOORE

1

"I bite into an apple & then get bored
before the second bite," you said.
You were also Samson. I had cut
your hair & locked you up.
Besides, your room was bugged.
A former inmate left his muse
spread-eagled on the picture window.
In the glinting late-day sun
we saw her huge & cross-eyed breasts appear
diamond-etched
against the slums of Harlem.
You tongued your pills & cursed the residents.
You called me Judas.
You forgot I was a girl.

2

Your hands weren't birds. To call
them birds would be too easy.
They drew circles around your ideas
& your ideas were sometimes parabolas.
That sudden Sunday you awoke
& found yourself behind the looking glass
your hands perched on the breakfast table

waiting for a sign.
I had nothing to tell them.
They conversed with the eggs.

3

We walked.
Your automatic umbrella snapped
into place above your head
like a black halo.
We thought of climbing down rain puddles
as if they were manholes.
You said the reflected buildings
led to hell.
Trees danced for us,
cut-out people turned sideways
& disappeared into their voices.
The cities in our glasses took us in.
You stood on a scale, heard the penny drop—
but the needle was standing still!
It proved that you were God.

4

The elevator opens & reveals me
holding African violets.
An hour later I vanish
into a chasm whose dimensions
are 23 hours.
Tranquilized, brittle
you strut the corridors
among the dapper young psychiatrists,

the girls who weave rugs all day,
unravel them all night,
the obesity cases lost in themselves.
You hum. You say you hate me.
I would like to shake you.
Remember how it happened?
You were standing at the window
speaking about flying.
Your hands flew to my throat.
When they came they found
our arms strewn around the floor
like broken toys.
We both were crying.

5

You stick. Somewhere in a cellar of my mind,
you stick. Fruit spoke to you
before it spoke to me. Apples cried
when you peeled them.
Tangerines jabbered in Japanese.
You stared into an oyster
& sucked out God.
You were the hollow man,
with Milton entering your left foot.

6

My first husband!—God—
you've become an abstraction,
a kind of Idea. I can't even hear

your voice any more. Only the black hair
curled on your belly makes you real—
I draw black curls on all the men I write.
I don't even look anymore.

7

I thought of you in Istanbul.
Your Byzantine face,
thin lips & hollow cheeks,
the fanatical melting brown eyes.
In Hagia Sophia they're stripping down
the moslem plaster
to find mosaics underneath.
The pieces fit in place.
You'd have been a Saint.

8

I'm good at interiors.
Gossip, sharpening edges, kitchen poems—
& have no luck at all with maps.
It's because of being a woman
& having everything inside.
I decorated the cave,
hung it with animal skins & woolens,
such soft floors,
that when you fell
you thought you fell on me.
You had a perfect sense of bearings
to the end,
were always pointing North.

9

Flying you home—
good Christ—flying you home,
you were terrified.
You held my hand, I held
my father's hand & he
filched pills from the psychiatrist
who'd come along for you.
The psychiatrist was 26 & scared.
He hoped I'd keep you calm.
& so we flew.
Hand in hand in hand in hand we flew.

Narcissus, Photographer

*". . . a frozen memory, like any photo,
where nothing is missing, not even,
and especially, nothingness. . ."*
                    JULIO CORTÁZAR, "BLOW UP"

Mirror-mad,
he photographed reflections:
sunstorms in puddles,
cities in canals,

double portraits framed
in sunglasses,
the fat phantoms who dance
on the flanks of cars.

Nothing caught his eye
unless it bent
or glistered
over something else.

He trapped clouds in bottles
the way kids
trap grasshoppers.
Then one misty day

he was stopped
by the windshield.
Behind him,
an avenue of trees,

before him,
the mirror of that scene.
He seemed to enter
what, in fact, he left.

Flower Eaters

"*Browning wrote to his friend that he would sometimes bite flowers and leaves to bits 'in an impatience at being unable to possess myself of them thoroughly, to see them quite, to satiate myself with their scent.'*"

Browning, you make me want
a nineteenth-century mouth
(greater, I mean, than the sum
of its devourings)
because I am trying, trying
to sidle the iris between slick teeth,
to tongue the crocuses and roses—
but it's no use.
They've cut off my honey.
Does my tongue no longer love me?
(Did it ever?)
No longer mother me?
Its hunger runs on, runs on.
Its anger!
Meanwhile you're gorging on pink petals
& waxy white pistils
(and the kids protest that they've discovered flowers!)
& I sit here wondering:
how many have devoured the world?
how much remains?
Despite the various subtle forms of lockjaw
(despite this tongue so stubbornly stuck in my cheek),
can poetry still enter through the mouth?
Nowadays, who can afford
a nineteenth-century mouth?
Roethke arrived and the greenhouse revolted.

New blooms fought up like Robespierres.
Orchids were "adder-mouthed,"
the roses appalling,
the cyclamen suddenly sneaky.
Old weed-puller, old fearer.
You tried to breathe the dirt.
(It filled your mouth.)
You never died,
you just stopped hungering.
Sylvia kept bees & they kept her
(thinking to learn the honey-sucking secrets).
Flowers were animal mouths, devourers
growing up toward a father who blazed like the sun.
In the end, your daughter fled
to the heart of the hive.

Browning, you wouldn't believe it.
The flowers have had us.
I try to take the roses with my teeth.
I suck for honey & gulp air.
Dear Browning, put on your hat,
your Victorian hat.
Put on your mouth, your gestures.
Put a flower in your mouth.
Only a hundred years and yet,
we don't eat flowers any more.
It works
the other way around.

You Operate

You operate on the afternoon
You perform open heart surgery
on the ghosts
of your suicidal friends

You divorce your parents
before you have time
to be born

You kick out your wife & child
You tell your girlfriend
to go screw herself

This is the solitude you wanted
The silence
is stitching you up
you write

Books

"The universe (which others call the library)..."
JORGE LUIS BORGES

Books which are stitched up the center with coarse white
thread
Books on the beach with sunglass-colored pages
Books about food with pictures of weeping grapefruits
Books about baking bread with browned corners
Books about long-haired Frenchmen with uncut pages
Books of erotic engravings with pages that stick
Books about inns whose stars have sputtered out
Books of illuminations surrounded by darkness
Books with blank pages & printed margins
Books with fanatical footnotes in no-point type
Books with book lice
Books with rice-paper pastings
Books with book fungus blooming over their pages
Books with pages of skin with flesh-colored bindings
Books by men in love with the letter O
Books which smell of earth whose pages turn

The Book

I float down the spiral stairs
of the old apartment.
At the dining room table sit
my six ex-analysts, two brokers,
& five professors,
considering my book.
They dip the pages of the manuscript in water,
to see if it will last.

From where I watch, the sheets look blank.

They discuss my sexual hang-ups.
Why do I write about women
when, after all, they're men?
They enumerate my debts, losses,
& the lies I've told; the red lights
I have passed, the men I've kissed.

They examine a lock of my hair for bleach.

Finally, muttering, they rise & yawn in chorus.
They decide to repossess my typewriter, my legs,
my Phi Beta Kappa key, one breast,
any children I may have,
& my espresso machine.

My book, of course, is through.
Already the pages have dissolved like toilet paper.

I wake up with the bed
still on the wrong side of the dream.
My legs are scattered through the streets
like pick-up sticks.

Crawling on stumps, crawling
in the spittle & dog shit,
I bitterly accuse the City
& bitterly accuse myself.

How could I not have known
that the book was on the wrong side
of the dream?
How could I
have walked into it?

Where It Begins

The corruption begins with the eyes,
the page, the hunger.
It hangs on the first hook
of the first comma.

The mouth shuts & opens.
Newspapers are there & nursery rhymes.
Readers, lovers dangle
like Cassius, Brutus
from Satan's teeth.

The corruption begins with the mouth,
the tongue, the wanting.
The first poem in the world
is *I want to eat.*

The breast is the screen
of the dream;
no hungry poet
can ever be content
with two.

The corruption begins with the breasts,
the cunt, the navel.
It begins with wanting love
from strangers.

The breasts are two blind animals
with painted eyes.

The cunt is a furry deaf mute
speaking a red tongue.
The tongue is hunger.

The corruption begins with the curled snail
of the baby.
It begins with the white flood
of love on pages.

It begins with emptiness
where love begins.
It begins with love
where emptiness
begins.

HALF-LIVES

For my mother & father

The notion of emptiness generates passion.
THEODORE ROETHKE

Contents

PROLOGUE/*The Evidence*

1

Evidence of life:
snapshots,
hundreds of split-seconds
when the eyes glazed over,
the hair stopped its growing,
the nails froze in fingertips,
the blood hung suspended
in its vessels—

while the small bloodships,
the red & white bloodboats
buoyed up & down at anchor
like the toys
of millionaires. ...

Evidence of life:
a split-second's death
to live forever
in something called
a *print*.
A paparazzo life:
I shoot therefore I am.

2

Why does life need evidence
of life?
We disbelieve it
even as we live.

The bloodboats gently rocking,
the skull opening every night
to dreams more vivid than itself,
more solid
than its own bones,
the brain flowering with petals,
stamens, pistils,
magical fruit
which reproduces
from its own juice,
which invents
its own mouth,
& makes itself anew
each night.

3

Evidence of life?
My dreams.
The dreams which I write down.
The dreams which I relate
each morning with a solemn face
inventing as I go.

Evidence of life:
that we could meet for the first time,
open our scars & stitches to each other,
weave our legs around
each other's patchwork dreams

& try to salve each other's wounds
with love—

if it was love.

(I am not sure at all
if love is salve
or just
a deeper kind of wound.
I do not think it matters.)

If it was lust or hunger
& not love,
if it was all that they accused us of
(that we accused ourselves)—
I do not think it matters.

4

Evidence of love?
I imagine our two heads
sliced open like grapefruits,
pressed each half to half
& mingling acid juice
in search of sweet.

I imagine all my dreams
sliding out into your open skull—
as if I were the poet,
you the reader.

I imagine all your dreams
pressed against my belly
like your sperm
& singing into me.

I imagine my two hands
cupped around your life
& stroking it.

I imagine your two hands
making whirlpools
in my blood,
then quelling them.

5

I have no photograph of you.
At times I hardly can believe in you.
Except this ache,
this longing in my gut,
this emptiness which theorizes you
because if there is emptiness this deep,
there must be fullness somewhere.

My other half!
My life beyond this half-life!

Is life a wound
which dreams of being healed?

Is love a wound which deepens
as it dreams?

Do you exist?
Evidence:
these poems in which
I have been conjuring you,
this book which makes your absence palpable,
these longings printed black.

132 /

I am exposed.
I am a print of darkness
on a square of film.
I am a garbled dream
told by a breakfast-table liar.
I am a wound which has forgotten how to heal.

6

& if it wasn't love,
if you called me now
across the old echo chamber of the ocean
& said:
"Look, I never loved you,"
I would feel
a little like a fool perhaps,
& yet it wouldn't matter.

My business is to always feel
a little like a fool
& speak of it.

& I am sure
that when we love
we are better than ourselves
& when we hate,
worse.

& even if we call it madness later
& scrawl four-letter words
across those outhouse walls
we call our skulls—
we stand revealed

by those sudden moments
when we come together.

7

Evidence?
Or was it just my dream
waltzing with your dream?
My nightmare kissing yours?

When I awakened
did I walk with Jacob's limp?
Did I sing a different song?
Did I find the inside of my palm
scarred as if
(for moments) it held fire?
Did my blood flow as riverwater flows
around a tree stump—
crooked, with a lilt?

What other evidence
did I need?

I/THE WIVES OF MAFIOSI

*Two habits have taught me how to keep
back my tears: the habit of concealing
my thoughts, and that of darkening my
lashes with mascara.*

COLETTE

*I have to thank God I'm a woman
for in these ordered days a woman only
is free to be very hungry, very lonely.*

ANNA WICKHAM

*(She died of internal
weeping.)*
ELEANOR ROSS TAYLOR

Climbing You

I want to understand the steep thing
that climbs ladders in your throat.
I can't make sense of you.
Everywhere I look you're there—
a vast landmark, a volcano
poking its head through the clouds,
Gulliver sprawled across Lilliput.

I climb into your eyes, looking.
The pupils are black painted stage flats.
They can be pulled down like window shades.
I switch on a light in your iris.
Your brain ticks like a bomb.

In your offhand, mocking way
you've invited me into your chest.
Inside: the blur that poses as your heart.
I'm supposed to go in with a torch
or maybe hot water bottles
& defrost it by hand
as one defrosts an old refrigerator.
It will shudder & sigh
(the icebox to the insomniac).

Oh there's nothing like love between us.
You're the mountain, I am climbing you.
If I fall, you won't be all to blame,
but you'll wait years maybe
for the next doomed expedition.

Seventeen Warnings in Search of a Feminist Poem

for Aaron Asher

1   Beware of the man who denounces ambition;
         his fingers itch under his gloves.

2   Beware of the man who denounces war
         through clenched teeth.

3   Beware of the man who denounces women writers;
         his penis is tiny & cannot spell.

4   Beware of the man who wants to protect you;
         he will protect you from everything but
                           himself.

5   Beware of the man who loves to cook;
         he will fill your kitchen with greasy pots.

6   Beware of the man who loves your soul;
         he is a bullshitter.

7   Beware of the man who denounces his mother;
         he is a son of a bitch.

8   Beware of the man who spells son of a bitch as one
                           word;
         he is a hack.

9   Beware of the man who loves death too well;
         he is taking out insurance.

10   Beware of the man who loves life too well;
         he is a fool.

11 Beware of the man who denounces psychiatrists;
       he is afraid.

12 Beware of the man who trusts psychiatrists;
       he is in hock.

13 Beware of the man who picks your dresses;
       he wants to wear them.

14 Beware of the man you think is harmless;
       he will surprise you.

15 Beware of the man who cares for nothing but books;
       he will run like a trickle of ink.

16 Beware of the man who writes flowery love letters;
       he is preparing for years of silence.

17 Beware of the man who praises liberated women;
       he is planning to quit his job.

The Wives of Mafiosi

Thinking to take on the power
       of a dark suit lined with lead
       of a man with a platinum mouth & knuckles of
                                  brass
       of a bullet the color of a Ferrari

the wives of Mafiosi stay home
decanting the Chianti
like transparent blood.

They crochet spiders for the furniture.
They go to Confession.
They fill the ears of the priests
with mozzarella & nougat candy.

We too stay home
& dream of power.
       We sacrifice the steakblood to the dishwasher.
       We bring clear offerings of water to the plants.
       We pray before the baby pictures.

We dream of swallowing bullets
& coupling with money.
       We dream of transparent armor.
       We imagine we want peace.
       We imagine we are different
       from the wives of Mafiosi.

Anniversary

Every night for five years
he chewed on her
until her fingers were red & ragged
until blue veins hung out of her legs
until the children tumbled
like baby kangaroos
out of raw crimson pouches
in her stomach.

Now she was done.
She had once been a woman.
She had once sprinkled perfume
from the split ends of her hair.
She had once left a silver trail of sequins
in the moonlight
& slipped between the clouds.
She had once sucked
on inky fingers at school
& drawn a perfect india ink man.
She had once prayed to movie stars & poets.
She had once cried into the *Rubaiyat*.
She had once worshipped swizzle sticks from Birdland
& dreamed of a man with perfect teeth
& a wedding in a carved block of ice.

Divorce

Eggs boiling in a pot.
They click
like castanets.
I put one in a cup
& slice its head off.

Under the wobbly egg white
is my first husband.
Look how small he's grown
since last we met!

"Eat me," he says agreeably.
I hesitate, then bite.

The thick yolk runs down
my thighs.

I take another egg
& slice its head.
Inside is my second husband.
This one's better done.

"You liked the white," I say,
"I liked the yolk."

He doesn't speak
but scowls as if to say:
"Everyone always eats me
in the end."

I chew him up
but I spit out

his jet-black hair,
the porcelain jackets from his teeth,
his cufflinks, fillings,
eyeglass frames. . . .

I drink my coffee
& I read the *Times*.

Another egg is boiling in the pot.

Paper Cuts

for Bob Phillips

Endless duplication of lives and objects . . .
THEODORE ROETHKE

I have known the imperial power of secretaries,
the awesome indifference of receptionists,
I have been intimidated by desk & typewriter,
by the silver jaws of the stapler
& the lecherous kiss of the mucilage,
& the unctuousness of rubber cement
before it dries.

I have been afraid of telephones,
have put my mouth to their stale tobacco breath,
have been jarred to terror
by their jangling midnight music,
& their sudden blackness
even when they are white.

I have been afraid in elevators
amid the satin hiss of cables
& the silky lisping of air conditioners
& the helicopter blades of fans.
I have seen time killed in the office jungles
of undeclared war.

My fear has crept into the paper guillotine
& voyaged to the Arctic Circle of the water cooler.
My fear has followed me into the locked Ladies Room,
& down the iron fire stairs
to the postage meter.

I have seen the mailroom women like lost letters
frayed around the edges.
I have seen the xerox room men
shuffling in & out among each other
like cards in identical decks.

I have come to tell you I have survived.
I bring you chains of paperclips instead of emeralds.
I bring you lottery tickets instead of poems.
I bring you mucilage instead of love.

I lay my body out before you on the desk.
I spread my hair amid a maze of rubber stamps.
RUSH. SPECIAL DELIVERY. DO NOT BEND.
I am open—will you lick me like an envelope?
I am bleeding—will you kiss my paper cuts?

Why I Died

She is the woman I follow.
Whenever I enter a room
she has been there—

    with her hair smelling of lions & tigers,
    with her dress blacker than octopus ink,
    with her shoes moving like lizards
    over the waving wheat of the rug.

Sometimes I think of her as my mother
but she died by her own hand
before I was born.

    She drowned in the waves of her own hair.
    She strangled on Isadora's scarf.
    She suckled a poisonous snake at her breast
    like Cleopatra or Eve.

She is no virgin & no madonna.
Her eyelids are purple.
She sleeps around.

    Wherever I go I meet her lovers.
    Wherever I go I hear their stories.
    Wherever I go they tell me
    different versions of her suicide.

I sleep with them in gratitude.
I sleep with them to make them tell.
I sleep with them as punishment or reward.

She is the woman I follow.
I wear her cast-off clothes.
She is my mother, my daughter.
She is writing this suicide note.

How You Get Born

One night, your mother is listening to the walls.
The clock whirrs like insect wings.
The ticking says lonely lonely lonely.

In the living room, the black couch swallows her.
She trusts it more than men,
but no one will ever love her
enough.

She doesn't yet know you
so how can she love you?
She loves you like God or Shakespeare.
She loves you like Mozart.

You are trembling in the walls like music.
You cross the ceiling in a phantom car of light.

Meanwhile unborn,
you wait in a heavy rainsoaked cloud
for your father's thunderbolt.
Your mother lies in the living room dreaming your hands.
Your mother lies in the living room dreaming your eyes.

She awakens & a shudder shakes her teeth.
The world is beginning again after the flood.

She slides into bed beside that gray-faced man,
your father.
She opens her legs to your coming.

Babyfood

They made the child so they could touch each other.

His breasts grew round, his belly swelled,
her navel sent a vine to meet his own,
& they took root in each other.

"We are pregnant," they would say,
talking to friends.

& she would pat his belly
& pull in her own.

Between his father's legs
the child first saw the world.
It was mountainous & cold.

The women marched together
carrying guns.
The men stayed home & wept.

Now his breasts give milk,
his tears turn into food.
The child is fed on tears just as before.

They made the child to open doors into themselves.

They closed them.
They fed him milk & tears.

Men

(*after a poem called "Women" by Nicanor Parra*)

The impossible man
The man with the ebony penis ten feet tall
The man of pentelikon marble
The man with the veined bronze figleaf which comes
                                        unhinged
The man who's afraid to get pregnant
The man who screws in his socks
The man who screws in his glasses
The man who screws in his sunglasses
The man who gets married a virgin
The man who marries a virgin
The man who wilts out of guilt
The man who adores his mother
The man who makes it with fruit
The husband who never has time
The husband who'd rather have power
The poet who'd rather have boys
The conductor who loves his baton
The analyst who writes "poems"
All these Adonises
All these respectable gents
Those descended
& those undescended
will drive me out of my skull sooner or later

Alcestis on the Poetry Circuit

(IN MEMORIAM *Marina Tsvetayeva,*
Anna Wickham, Sylvia Plath, Shakespeare's
sister, etc., etc.)

The best slave
does not need to be beaten.
She beats herself.

Not with a leather whip,
or with sticks or twigs,
not with a blackjack
or a billyclub,
but with the fine whip
of her own tongue
& the subtle beating
of her mind
against her mind.

For who can hate her half so well
as she hates herself?
& who can match the finesse
of her self-abuse?

Years of training
are required for this.
Twenty years
of subtle self-indulgence,
self-denial;
until the subject
thinks herself a queen
& yet a beggar—
both at the same time.
She must doubt herself
in everything but love.

She must choose passionately
& badly.
She must feel lost as a dog
without her master.
She must refer all moral questions
to her mirror.
She must fall in love with a cossack
or a poet.

She must never go out of the house
unless veiled in paint.
She must wear tight shoes
so she always remembers her bondage.
She must never forget
she is rooted in the ground.

Though she is quick to learn
& admittedly clever,
her natural doubt of herself
should make her so weak
that she dabbles brilliantly
in half a dozen talents
& thus embellishes
but does not change
our life.

If she's an artist
& comes close to genius,
the very fact of her gift
should cause her such pain
that she will take her own life
rather than best us.

& after she dies, we will cry
& make her a saint.

The Critics

*(For everyone who writes about
Sylvia Plath including me)*

Because she was clamped in the vise of herself
because she was numb
because words moved slowly as glaciers
because they flowed from her mouth like wine
because she was angry
& knotted her hair
& wore sand in her bra
because she had written herself into a corner
& could not get out
because she had painted the sun on her ceiling
& then got burned
because she invented the stars
& watched them fall . . .

There is nothing to say now.
You have filled her grave with your theories,
her eyes with your sights.
You have picked her bones clean
as ancestor bones.
They could not gleam whiter.
But she is gone.
She is grass you have trod.
She is dust you have blown away.

She sits in her book like an aphid,
small & white.
She is patient.
When you're silent
she'll crawl out.

Three Sisters

They will never get to Moscow.
They sit on a brown hilltop dangling their feet
into the blue pages of the sky.

One can't stand a house without a baby.
One is handcuffed to a typewriter.
The youngest sits in the center chiding the clouds.

Here is the inside of the dream bus.
The walls are made of clouds that look like glass.
Each in her own way has tried to get in.
But the way was blocked
by quarrels, baby bottles, charge accounts of guilt
& the sour smell of money.

The one with the typewriter rattles her chains & handcuffs.
If only they'd leap onto the keys (she thinks)
they'd learn to dance
If only they'd wrap themselves in dust-jackets
before they die.

The oldest delivers her fourth baby into the sky.
The youngest blames the sky.

The Man Who Can Only Paint Death

A man who does not believe in women
believes in death.
He has painted it rising with bone wings
over the dark of his house.
He has sung to it in a pale monotone.
He has stroked its hair.

But his hand comes back covered with cobwebs
& his throat fills with dust.
The bone wings creak when he raises his brush.
His wife turns in her bed.

He dreams of his mother's grave going to seed.
He smells the dust of her hair.
He is the gray flower which grows
between her headstone & the sky.
He is the weed in the paving crack.
He is the baby in black.

His daughter turns & turns in her sleep.
Her eyelids move with dreams.
She dreams she awakens & finds him gone,
& her grandmother's name is death.

The Widower

She left him in death's egg,
the bone sack & the gunny sack,
the bag of down & feathers—all black. . . .
Somehow he couldn't get back.

It was night,
a night of shark-faced jets
winking brighter than blue stars,
a night of poisoned cities
mushrooming beneath the eyes of jets,
a night of missile silos
sulking in the desert,
a night of babies howling in the alleys,
a night of cats.

She left a death so huge
his life got lost in it.
She left a bloodstained egg
he had to hatch.

Back to Africa

Among the Gallas, when a woman grows tired
of the cares of housekeeping, she begins to
talk incoherently and demean herself extravagantly.
This is a sign of the descent of the holy spirit
Callo upon her. Immediately, her husband prostrates
himself and adores her; she ceases to bear the humble
title of wife and is called "Lord"; domestic duties
have no further claim on her, and her will is a divine law.

SIR JAMES GEORGE FRAZIER,
The Golden Bough

Seeing me weary
    of patching the thatch
    of pounding the bread
    of pacing the floor nightly
    with the baby in my arms,

my tall black husband
    (with eyes like coconuts)
    has fallen down on the floor to adore me!
    I curse myself for being born a woman.
    He thinks I'm God!

I mutter incoherently of Friedan, Millett, Freud. . . .
    He thinks the spirit
    has descended.
    He calls me "Lord."

Lord, lord, he's weary in his castle now.
    It's no fun living with a God.
    He rocks the baby, patches thatch
    & pounds the bread.
    I stay out all night with the Spirit.

Towards morning when the Spirit brings me home,
    he's almost too pooped to adore me.
    I lecture him on the nature
    & duties of men.
    "Biology is destiny," I say.

Already I hear stirrings of dissent.
    He says he could have been a movie star.
    He says he needs a full-time maid.
    He says he never *meant*
    to marry God.

Mother

Ash falls on the roof
of my house.

I have cursed you enough
in the lines of my poems
& between them,
in the silences which fall
like ash-flakes
on the watertank
from a smog-bound sky.

I have cursed you
because I remember
the smell of *Joy*
on a sealskin coat
& because I feel
more abandoned than a baby seal
on an ice floe red
with its mother's blood.

I have cursed you
as I walked & prayed
on a concrete terrace
high above the street
because whatever I pulled down
with my bruised hand
from the bruising sky,
whatever lovely plum
came to my mouth
you envied
& spat out.

Because you saw me in your image,
because you favored me,
you punished me.

It was only a form of you
my poems were seeking.
Neither of us knew.

For years
we lived together
in a single skin.

We shared fur coats.
We hated each other
as the soul hates the body
for being weak,
as the mind hates the stomach
for needing food,
as one lover hates the other.

I kicked
in the pouch of your theories
like a baby kangaroo.

I believed you
on Marx, on Darwin,
on Tolstoy & Shaw.
I said I loved Pushkin
(you loved him).
I vowed Monet
was better than Bosch.

Who cared?

I would have said nonsense
to please you
& frequently did.

This took the form,
of course,
of fighting you.

We fought so gorgeously!

We fought like one boxer
& his punching bag.
We fought like mismatched twins.
We fought like the secret sharer
& his shade.

Now we're apart.
Time doesn't heal
the baby to the womb.
Separateness is real
& keeps on growing.

One by one the mothers
drop away,
the lovers leave,
the babies outgrow clothes.

Some get insomnia—
the poet's disease—
& sit up nights
nursing
at the nipples
of their pens.

I have made hot milk
& kissed you where you are.
I have cursed my curses.
I have cleared the air.
& now I sit here writing,
breathing you.

The Girl in the Mirror

Throwing away my youth on duty
        on ink, on guilt,
        on applications ...

I thought of you
        in your mirrored room,
        you with the huge open heart
        pulsing like a womb which has just given birth,
        pulsing like the beat in my head
        before a poem starts.

I thought of you
        & your charmed life,
        your hassocks, waterbeds & sliding mirrors,
        your closets full of beautiful faces,
        & your men, your men

the way you could open & close
        your legs without guilt,
        the way you said yes & yes & yes,
        the way you dealt death & regret
        as if they were cards,
        the way you asked nothing
        & everything came to you

Remember how we both loved
        that girl from the Kingdom of Oz?*

She had thirty heads—all beautiful—
        but just one dress.

*Princess Langwidere in L. Frank Baum's *Ozma of Oz*.

She kept her heads in a mirrored cupboard
    opened with a ruby key.
    It was chained to her wrist.

She had my heart chained to her wrist!
    I wanted to *be* her.

Though some of her heads were mad
    she could never remember which
    until she wore them,
    & one had a terrible temper,
    & one loved blood.

Can you imagine a girl
    who put on the wrong head one day
    & killed her body by mistake?

Can you imagine a girl
    who would not believe she was beautiful
    & kept opening her legs to the wrong men?

Can you imagine a girl
    who cut off her head
    to get rid of the guilt?

But no:

    you are lying in a room
    where everything is silver.
    The ceiling is mirrored,
    the floor is mirrored,
    & men come out of the walls.

One by one, they make love to you
    like princes climbing a glass mountain.
    They admire your faces
    & the several colors of your hair.

They admire your smooth pink feet
& your hands which have never known ink.
They kiss your fingers.

You are everywhere.
You can come all night
& never tire.

Your voices mist the mirrors
but you never write.

You have my children
& they fugue the world.

Someday when my work is done
I'll come to you.

No one will be the wiser.

Regret

for Mimi Bailin

Regret is the young girl who sits in the snow
& stares at her hands.

They are bluer than shadows in snow.
They are bloodless as fear.
Her fingernail moons are white.

She wants to crawl into the palm
of her own hand.
She wants extra fingers to cover
the shame of her eyes.

She wants to follow her lifeline where it leads
but it plunges deeper
than the Grand Canyon.

She stands on the edge
still hoping
she can fly.

II/A CRAZY SALAD

It's certain that fine women eat
A crazy salad with their meat
Whereby the horn of plenty is undone.
WILLIAM BUTLER YEATS

Even his heart wishes to bite apples.
THEODORE ROETHKE

The Eggplant Epithalamion

for Grace & David Griffin

> *"Mostly you eat eggplant at least once a day," she explained. "A Turk won't marry a woman unless she can cook eggplant at least a hundred ways."*
> ARCHAEOLOGIST IRIS LOVE, SPEAKING OF THE CUISINE ON DIGS IN TURKEY. *The New York Times*, February 4, 1971

1

There are more than a hundred Turkish poems
about eggplant.
I would like to give you all of them.
If you scoop out every seed,
you can read me backward
like an Arabic book.
Look.

2

(Lament in Aubergine)

Oh aubergine,
egg-shaped
& as shiny as if freshly laid—
you are a melancholy fruit.
Solanum Melongena.
Every animal is sad
after eggplant.

3

(Byzantine Eggplant Fable)

Once upon a time on the coast of Turkey
there lived a woman who could cook eggplant 99 ways.

She could slice eggplant thin as paper.
She could write poems on it & batter-fry it.
She could bake eggplant & broil it.
She could even roll the seeds in banana-
flavored cigarette papers
& get her husband high on eggplant.
But he was not pleased.
He went to her father & demanded his bride-price back.
He said he'd been cheated.

He wanted back two goats, twelve chickens
& a camel as reparation.
His wife wept & wept.
Her father raved.

The next day she gave birth to an eggplant.
It was premature & green
& she had to sit on it for days
before it hatched.
"This is my hundredth eggplant recipe," she screamed.
"I hope you're satisfied!"

(Thank Allah that the eggplant was a boy.)

4

(*Love & the Eggplant*)

On the warm coast of Turkey, Miss Love
eats eggplant
"at least once a day."

How fitting that love should eat eggplant,
that most aphrodisiac fruit.

Fruit of the womb
of Asia Minor,

reminiscent of eggs,
of Istanbul's deep purple nights
& the Byzantine eyes of Christ.

I remember the borders of egg & dart
fencing us off from the flowers & fruit
of antiquity.
I remember the egg & tongue
probing the lost scrolls of love.
I remember the ancient faces
of Aphrodite
hidden by dust
in the labyrinth under
the British Museum
to be finally found by Miss Love
right there
near Great Russell Square.

I think of the hundreds of poems of the eggplant
& my friends who have fallen in love
over an eggplant,
who have opened the eggplant together
& swum in its seeds,
who have clung in the egg of the eggplant
& have rocked to sleep
in love's dark purple boat.

The Woman Who Loved to Cook

Looking for love, she read cookbooks,
She read recipes for *tartlettes*,
terrines de boeuf, timbales,
& Ratatouille.
She read cheese fondue
& Croque Monsieur,
& Hash High Brownies
& Lo Mein.

If no man appeared who would love her
(her face moist with cooking,
her breasts full of apple juice
or wine),
she would whip one up:
of gingerbread,
with baking powder
to make him rise.

Even her poems
were recipes.
"Hunger," she would write, "hunger."
The magic word to make it go away.
But nothing filled her up
or stopped that thump.
Her stomach thought it was a heart.

Then one day she met a man,
his cheeks brown as gingerbread,
his tongue a slashed pink ham
upon a platter.
She wanted to eat him whole
& save his eyes.
Her friends predicted he'd eat her.

How does the story end?
You know it well.

She's getting fatter
& she drinks too much.

Her shrink has read her book
& heard her tale.

"Oral," he says,
& coughs
& puffs his pipe.

"Oral,"
he says,
& now
"time's up."

The Bait

(*with apologies to Sir Walter Raleigh,
Christopher Marlowe, John Donne, et al.*)

The poet of sulks.
I had often seen him at a bar,
or at a reading,
sulking through the smoke.

In his pocket
a manuscript crackled
giving off
an acrid smell.

"If they'd shut up,"
his scowl seemed to say,
"I'd show them all
what poetry's about."

I swear his meanness turned me on.
I took him home.

I fed him rice & shrimps & cheesecake
& white wine.
I tickled his tongue with puns.

The poet of sulks
would have none of this.
He called me trivial
because I like to laugh.

He laid me once & then attacked
my poems & cooking—
which he'd got confused.

174 /

"Your cheesecake poem is rather rich,"
he grudged.
"Your rice is overdone."

I saw that I'd get nowhere
with this guy.
So I began to sulk.

After an hour or two
he finally caught on.

"What's bugging you?"
he asked.

"I'm waiting for the sky to fall,"
I gloomed.
"I'm waiting for the Apocalypse
to fuck me from behind."

"Do you really think it will?"
he asked.
"I'm sure of it,"
I said.

"Come live with me & be my love," said he.

Chinese Food

The mouth is an unlimited measure.
CHINESE PROVERB

Won Ton Soup

The soup contains something from each moment
of your life.
It is hot & sour.
There are islands of chives floating
like green ideas in the mind.
There is the won ton folded
like an embryo
skimming the water
waiting to be born.
There are the small unkosher bits of pork,
forbidden foods
which promise all the flavor.
There are the crystal noodles:
threads of silver light.

You eat your life
out of a skull-shaped bowl.
You eat it
with a porcelain spoon.
It is dense as water.
It is sour as death.
It is hot as an adulterous love.
& the pork—forbidden both by Moses & Mohammed—
is pink & sweet.

Entree

For the next course we chose
1 from Column A
2 from Column B
4 from Column C
& we passed the plates around
to share our lives.

We wanted to say: Look—
you taste my portion,
I'll taste yours.

We wanted to say: Look—
I am dying of malnutrition.
Let's eat each other.

We wanted to say: Look—
I am tired of eating myself
every night
& every morning.
I am frightened
of my own mouth
which wants to devour me.
I am tired of the tapeworms
of my soul.

Belle ordered spareribs
sweet & sour.
"I have given my life to men,"
she said.
Like Eve in the garden
she chewed the rib
& regretted nothing.

Allan ate his beef with oyster sauce
& did not apologize
to Jews or Hindus.
"Sometimes food is only food,"
he said.

Roland ordered vegetables
& crunched
& spoke of meter.

Lucas ordered chicken
& denounced analysis.

Betty ordered dumplings
& defended it.

While Neal & Susan
dug deep
into their noodles.

I was left with sweet & sour pork,
haloed in batter,
glowing red with sauce,
slick as guilt
& sweet as smashed taboos.

Then we all poured tea.

Fortune Cookies

The man who chews on his woman
will be poisoned by her gall.

The woman who chews on her man
will end her days as a toothless hag.

The poet who writes of food
will never go hungry.

The poet who describes her friends at table
will eat her words.

The poet who writes on rice paper
will nourish her critics.

A poem about food will not feed
the starving nations.

Your own mouth will eat you
if you don't watch out.

On the Air

[*He*] *went entirely mad and had the delusion his penis was
a radio station....*

THEODORE ROETHKE IN CLASS,
QUOTED BY ALLEN SEAGER IN *The Glass House*

One toe
is the sensitive tip
of an iceberg,
& the moon sets
in my pinkie nail.
Every hair on my head
is transmitting signals.
My nipples give off
ultrasonic bleeps.

Only mad dogs
& lovers hear them.
Only distant poets
who are wired for sound.
He thinks his heart
is a receiving station.
His penis keeps on playing Rock & Roll.

I love a lunatic
whose feet are stereophonic.
His mustache tingles
like a tuning fork.
His fingers jangle
like a snail's antennae.
His navel rotates
like a radar screen.

Do you read me? Do you read me?
I keep asking.
When we're apart, when we're together
I keep asking.
& all the time he's spinning golden oldies.
His balls play Dixieland.
His foreskin honky tonk.

I play the engineer to his disk jockey.
I signal him to take a station break.
I ask him to identify the network.
I tell him to stop censoring the news.

It's Rock & Roll & Soul
& Body Counts.
It's pimple cream & soda pop
& jazz.
He thinks the FCC
has got his number.
He blames the President
when signals come in weak.
He thinks J. Edgar Hoover
sends him static.
& when he wilts,
he blames the FBI.

The Send-Off

for Patricia Goedicke & Leonard Robinson

(A letter to friends after sending the first book to the printer)

1

(Singing the Monthly Blues)

The book gone to the printer to die
& the flat-bellied author
disguised as me
is sick of the anger of being a woman
& sick of the hungers
& sick of the confessional poem of the padded bra
& the confessional poem of the tampax
& the bad-girl poets
who menstruate black ink.

I am one!
Born from my father's head
disguised as a daughter
angry at spoons & pots
with a half-life of men behind me
& a half-life of me ahead
with holes in my shoes
& holes in my husbands
& only the monthly flow of ink to keep me sane
& only sex to keep me pure.

I want to write about something other than women!
I want to write about something other than men!
I want stars in my open hand
& a house round as a pumpkin
& children's faces forming in the roots of trees.

2

Instead
I read my fortune in the bloodstains on the sheet.

3

What I wanted was something enormous,
a banyan tree
sinking its roots in the ground,
something green & complex as a trellis
eating the air
& the leaves uncurling their fingers
& the tendrils
reaching out for the wisps of my hair
& breathing the transformation.
To become a tree-girl!
with birds nesting in my navel
& poems sprouting from my fingertips—
but a tree with a voice.

4

I had imagined at least
an underground temple:
the Temple to Juno at Paestum,
the bone-jars & the honey-jars
& sacrifices sweetening the earth.

Instead: this emptiness.
The hollow of the book resounding
like an old well
in a ruined city.
No honey pot,
but another *Story of O*.

5

Sometimes the sentimentalist
says to hell with words
& longs to dig ditches.
She writes of this longing, of course,
& you,
because you are her friends,
write back.

6

She wants to write happiness books
with you—
big black happiness books—
because you tell her the moon's in your shoes
because you've taken off each other's socks
& counted each other's toes
& kissed
the spaces in between
because you fall (giggling)
into each other's books & find
the pages skin
because your laughter's the most serious sound
she's heard in years
because when she hears you making love
across the wall
you're singing
possible possible possible
while she sits here
in her big black book
beating her fists against the covers
loving the way she hates herself
much too much
to stop.

7

Here is the bottom of the pool
where the octopus
feeding on herself
vows to stop talking
about how
she wants to stop talking
about feeding on herself.

8

She is so bored with her notebook.
She has taken to writing in colored inks.
Green nouns. Shocking pink verbs.
Her notebook is a Mardi Gras.
The Rorschach on the sheet is brown.

9

She comes back again & again to this:
sex.
No matter how hard they mock her,
no matter what kind of cunt they call her,
no matter how shocked her father & mother,
caught in their cloud bed,
caught as in a primal scene
choreographed by Disney,
she comes back
to the dance
against death.

10

They are sitting in an office high
above Madison Avenue

speaking earnestly of commas.
He loves the way she uses them:
little hooks
to snare his shirt-tails.
But he proposes, tactfully, one semicolon.
Does he dare?
"I love your stuff," he says.
Stiff blue pencil, he would fall on her,
revising everything.
Her paper dress tears off
& the layers of poems which are her skins
peel off.

She is a little font of tiny type.
She is ink.
She is that fine black trickle
running out the door.

Orphan

A dream of rejection
in which you are invited
to only the wrong parties—

& when you arrive
it seems you've forgotten your skin
& your mother is there
showing everyone baby pictures.

You still had your skin then!

Why do you feel like an orphan
flayed alive?

Wherever you go
they admire your smile,
the white teeth of your wisecracks,
the apple-red cheeks of your laugh.

How can they know that you cry into your hair
& mop the floor?
That you sweep the rug with your lashes?
That you lick the soles of your lover's feet
to keep them clean?

You always believe he will leave you.
You are always alone.
Even when he lies over you—
a ship plowing
the iceberg edges of your soul,

you are alone,
& only the hunger of being in love
appeases your hunger.

Oh orphan
casting filaments like Whitman's spider,
sending letters to the world on colored paper,
sending photographs & kisses,
care packages & carbon copies,
onion skin—
the only skin you have.

The Nose

for Louis Untermeyer, who knows

Nose thou art sick.
You perch on the face
like a discouraged phallic symbol.
You perch between the eyes
like a boring critic.
You perch above the mouth
like a twitch, a boil, a wart,
& you itch at embarrassing times
like lust.

Gogol knew you for elusiveness—
how, just when we *need* a nose—
pouf!—you disappear
into a snotty handkerchief
or loaf of bread.

Pinocchio, that little wooden prick,
that secret pudding-puller,
that school drop-out,
knew how you grow & grow
like a maypole
making the sheets a tent
for your three-ring circus,
you sad impossible clown

(even great noses—
Cyrano, de Gaulle—
have to play the clown,
cannot escape
the general fate of noses).

Starlets & unmarriageable girls
whose noses
are far too nubile
cut them off.
The Freudian squints at this
with his diagnosis:
Proboscis Envy.

Most men
find their noses short
& sneak around the locker room
looking for
different colored noses
in repose.
No happy man
is happy with his nose.

My kingdom for a nose!
cried Hamlet.
(Something was blue in Denmark
besides the cheese.)
Ophelia appeared
offering her lily-white snout,
but Hamlet longed to have his mama
blow his nose
(according to Ernest Jones).

He later perished
from his old friend's sword—
Shakespeare playing it,
as always,
to the hilt.

Tales about noses
are always (you see)
moral.

190 /

The nose is a very upright organ.
It gets its nose rubbed in the mud.
It sprouts with pimples
from our adolescent dreams.
It figures in a moral song
on Reindeer.
It speaks
in the Braille of blackheads
of our lust.

& meanwhile *Life*
shows me a gigantic photo
of tiny smell-stalks
like a bed of coral.
The nose is the oldest organ
in the animal kingdom.
The nose is the organ
of memory & desire.
Poets are bloodhounds
tracking with their noses.
The nose is life.
Poor Yorick
has no nose.

Castration of the Pen

The pen is an index finger
which has learned
to give milk
like a breast.

It is curious.
It explores
the cunts of girls.
It explores
& tells.

It is nourishing.
It can suckle babies
with the bluest,
blackest milk.

It is clever,
has an endless store
of anecdotes & fables.

It is logical,
can do research,
can put its tip
against your piglike nose,
can even say
FUCK YOU.

But unlike your finger
or your breast
your pen is fickle.
It writes speeches
for two rival politicians.

It endorses checks
from almost anyone.
It writes bad lines
& writes good ones
without caring
& leaves you
to sort out the mess.

By this time
you have gathered
that the pen's a symbol.

Is it breast?
Or is it penis?

Cut it off!

III/THE AGE OF EXPLORATION

The human spirit is prey to the most
astounding impulses. Man goes constantly in
fear of himself. His erotic urges terrify
him. The saint turns from the voluptuary
in alarm; she does not know that his
unacknowledgeable passions and her own
are really one.

GEORGES BATAILLE

Had we remained together
We could have become a silence.
YEHUDA AMICHAI

Autobiographical

The lover in these poems
is me;
the doctor,
Love.
He appears
as husband, lover
analyst & muse,
as father, son
& maybe even God
& surely death.

All this is true.

The man you turn to
in the dark
is many men.

This is an open secret
women share
& yet agree to hide
as if
they might then
hide it from themselves.

I will not hide.

I write in the nude.
I name names.
I am I.
The doctor's name is Love.

The Age of Exploration

Sailing into your chest,
the white ship of my body
parts
the sun-struck water
of your skin
the silvery waves
of your hair—

a miracle!
the Red Sea parting for Moses—

& we ride
on a bed high
as the *Queen Mary*
& I straddle
your tall red smokestack
like the ocean wind
moaning
in mid-Atlantic.

All around us
people are waving good-bye.

Your wives bobbing in tiny lifeboats,
your children
riding on singing dolphins,
my mother
reaving the water
in an angry speedboat
& shouting warnings
through a megaphone,
my father
coolly shooting clay pigeons

from the burning deck,
my husband
about to harpoon
a great white whale . . .

Abandon ship!
Abandon ship!

We aren't listening.

Last lovers on the *Titanic*,
galley slaves transfixed
by the master's whip,
Jews in steerage,
Spaniards in search of gold . . .

You are the firehose
on my burning deck,
the radar
in my fog,
the compass
in my starless night. . . .

You are the prow
of Columbus' ship
kissing the lip
of the new world.

Half-Life

The rock I danced on
looked for all the world like the sea.
The sea was stone.

Your eyes were green
as wings of horseflies . . .
almost as unclean.

They buzzed around my head
like my own dreams.
They thickened the air with kisses.

When I was nine,
I used to kiss my pillow
on the mouth
after I'd licked it wet.
How else find out
what "soul-kiss"
really meant?

"He puts his tongue
into your mouth."

I was amazed.

& yet our tongues are dancing
on the ocean.

Why does every fucking poem
mention the ocean?

The swell of the great sea mother?
The water babies in their amniotic fluid?
The sea salt taste of blood?

Love, blood—the flood of poems
as life creaks to a close.

The sky narrows to a point
as we make love.

This is a little death,
a pact,
a double suicide of sorts.

& I invent
tidal waves, atomic shocks,
the mushroom cloud of you
above the smoking chasm
that you leave in me.

Radioactive,
dangerous as stone,
you leave me bone dry, lonely in my cave.

I have compared you to atomic war.

& your half-life will linger
when both of us
are gone.

Knives

The women he has had are all faces
without eyes.
He has entered them blind
as a cut worm.
He has swum their oceans
like a wounded fish
looking for home.

At nights when he can't sleep,
he dreams of weaving
backward up that river
where the banks
are fringed with mouths,
& weedy hair
grows amid the dark crusts
of ancient blood.

Tonight, he is afraid & lonely
in a city of meat & knives.
I would go under his knife
& move so willingly
that his heart
might turn to butter
in his mouth.

The Tongue

I crouch under your tongue
like a lover afraid
of her own lie.
The tongue is the organ of love
& the organ of lying.
& the lie clings to the tongue;
the lie fills
the hungry mouth of the world.

I remember the sweet places
between your words
where my tongue probed.
I remember the brass clash
of cymbals
when your tongue
struck my nipple
I remember the purple sounds
of your tongue in my cunt.
Your tongue was the bell clapper
to my bell.

I remember your tongue
which rolled out
like a red carpet.
I remember your plushy royal purple
velvet tongue.
I remember your Nazi tongue
which hummed Wagner.
I remember your light & playful
Mozart tongue.

This poem is a gob of spittle,
a thin dribble.
It meant to speak all tongues,
it meant to sing.
But yours is in my mouth
& I am dumb.

Touch

The house of the body
is a stately manor
open for nothing
never to the public.

But
for the owner of the house,
the key-holder—
the body swings open
like Ali Baba's mountain
glistening with soft gold
& red jewels.

These cannot be stolen
or sold for money.
They only glisten
when the mountain opens
by magic
or its own accord.

The gold triangle of hair,
its gentle *ping*,
the pink quartz crystals
of the skin,
the ruby nipples,
the lapis
of the veins
that swim the breast . . .

The key-holder
is recognized
by the way he holds

the body.
He is recognized
by touch.

Touch is the first sense to awaken
after the body's little death
in sleep.
Touch is the first sense
to alert the raw red infant
to a world of pain.

The body glimmers
on its dark mountain
pretending ignorance of this.

The Cabala According to Thomas Alva Edison

All objects give off sparks

Your tongue, for example, enters my mouth
& sends electricity along my veins

When we embrace in your office, your secretary turns blue
As the base of a flame

Your fly zips up & down making the sound
of a struck match

Even a struck match gives off sparks

My nails on the back of your knees
give off sparks
your nails on my thighs

Thighs, in general, give off sparks
But even the fuzz on thighs
gives off sparks

Sparks, in general, make the world go round
(There are, for example, spark plugs)

Plugs, in general, give off sparks

In & Out: the current of the world

Paper Chains

The first snow of the year
& you lying between my breasts
in my husband's house
& the snow gently rising in my throat
like guilt,
& the windows frosting over
as if etched by acid.

You come from the desert
& have left a little sand
between my legs
where it rubs & rubs
& secretes a milky fluid,
finally a poem
or a pearl.

I am your oyster shell,
your mother of pearl
gleaming like oil on water
for two hours on a snowy day.

"Poets fall in love to write about it!"
I said in my brittle way,
& told you about other loves to tempt you
& heard your siren songs of old affairs.

I fall in love as a kind of research project.
You fall in love as some men go to war.

What tanks!
What bombs!
What storms of index cards!

I am binding up your legs with carbon ribbon.
I tie you to the bed with paper chains.

Gardener

I am in love with my womb
& jealous of it.

I cover it tenderly
with a little pink hat
(a sort of yarmulke)
to protect it from men.

Then I listen for the gentle *ping*
of the ovary:
a sort of cupid's bow
released.
I'm proud of that.
& the spot of blood
in the little hat
& the egg so small
I cannot see it
though I pray to it.

I imagine the inside
of my womb to be
the color of poppies
& bougainvillea
(though I've never seen it).

But I fear the barnacle
which might latch on
& not let go
& I fear the monster
who might grow
to bite the flowers
& make them swell & bleed.

So I keep my womb empty
& full of possibility.

Each month
the blood sheets down
like good red rain.

I am the gardener.
Nothing grows without me.

Going to School in Bed

If it is impossible to promise
absolute fidelity,
this is because
we learn so much geography
from the shifting of one body
on another.

If it is impossible to promise
absolute fidelity,
this is because
we learn so much history
from the lying of one body
on another.

If it is impossible to promise
absolute fidelity,
this is because
we learn so much psychology
from the dreaming of one body
of another.

Life writes so many letters
on the naked bodies of lovers.
What a tattoo artist!
What an ingenious teacher!

Is it any wonder we appear
like schoolchildren dreaming:
naked
& anxious to learn?

The Book with Four Backs

I put our books face to face
so they could talk.
They whispered about us.

I put yours on top of mine.
They would not mate.

Like poor dumb pandas in the London Zoo,
they would not come together.

I put them back to back.
They would not sleep.

I put them right side up to upside down.
They would not lick each other's wounds.

The night we met
you fed me fish eggs & dark beer.
We spoke of animals & Shakespeare.
You talked about acidic inks & papers.
You told me how our books digest themselves.

You laid the pages of your body over mine.
You printed my face with kisses.
The letters fell into a heap under the bed.
The sheets were dust.
The fish eggs swam our mouths.

Going Away

I thought that by going away
I would keep you.
I would fill myself up
with your absence.
My legs would close
around the smell of you.
My tongue would probe
the rainy air
& the whole sky
would be your mouth
& Hampstead Heath your tongue
& I face down
upon the grass
would tongue the sodden ground
& taste you there.

Instead,
I am on a plane
moving away from you.
The minutes sound
like jet-screams in my ears.
The hours lower into place
like landing gear.
We turn & bank
(the engines are my heart)
& we are in New York.

Dr. Love,
I thought you'd cure me.
I was lying on the couch
holding your hand.
You told me fear

was my disease.
& look—
I have been analyzed for years
& still
it brings me down.

Come back!
(I can say this having left you.)
We'll fuck so hard the world
will fall apart.

Your pink tongue's in my mouth.
It speaks for me.
I love this sickness more than life.
There is no cure.

Going Between

What will the lovers *do* with their letters?
All night they lie awake scribbling
on each other's brains,
collecting lines they have no place to keep,
collecting memories which dip & flutter
like the moth of his tongue
in her cunt's flame.

They send each other letters—
telepathic letters, notebook letters,
muttered subway letters,
love words offered on the toilet seat,
love words spoken to a spoon or pot,
love words spoken to a dog,
a husband even,
love words scattered everywhere
but where they mean to go.

The lovers need a go-between.
Sometimes all of life comes down
to the search for a go-between.

She is writing on the air
above her husband's head.
He is scratching his wife's ass
& writing to her.
The air is full of letters, letters, letters!

Western Union, Eastern Union—what can join them?
Not even telephones can save them,
nor the persistence of mailmen in rain & fog & sleet.
Their lives are letters which they cannot send.
Their love has no address.

The Purification

Because she loved her husband
she found a lover.
Because she betrayed her husband with false fidelity
she went to bed with her lover.
Because she was no longer falsely faithful
she now felt honest.
Because she was honest
she told her lover she loved him.
Because she was honest
she told her lover she also loved her husband.
Because she was honest
her dishonest lover left her.
Because her lover left her
she felt betrayed.
Because she felt betrayed
she went back to her husband.
Now they had something in common.

Eve on Riverside Drive

When they wrenched you
from my side—

my curved rib,
my bone,
my beauty—

it was as if the sun
were gouged from the sky
& the clouds
ran red.

A common sunset
over Riverside Drive.
Eden in smog.
The industrial wastes
of New Jersey,
the apartment towers of the Mafia,
the thick vaseline
of the sky.

& I aching
with loneliness
as if I had just had
an abortion
& you thousands of miles away.

They told the story
the other way around
(Adam forfeits rib;
Eve is born)—
Obvious irony.

Everyone knew
that women do the bearing;
men are born.

Juvenal God
writing the Bible
with his poison pen.

Cross out the lie!
Correct the blasphemy!

They wrenched you
from my side.
My blood poured down.
We both were born.
The pain belonged to me.

Sadder

Because I was sadder than you
to start with
I loved harder.

When I'm alone in my room
the objects breathe
like patients in a ward
for contagious diseases.

When I'm alone at night
the white ceiling presses down on me
like an iceberg
& brown leaves move like mice
under the bed.

You putter in your garden.
You are painting the prow of a boat
to launch on the Thames.
You are grinding coffee by hand
or lying under your car
as if under a woman.

Cooking or fucking,
you live in your skin.

I wander the world like an exile
& occasionally rest
on the shores of a poem.

But you were happier shoveling shit
than I was writing a poem

& that was hard.
I wanted to give up words
& stay with you.

I wanted to try.

But my sadness
was a stern husband.
He would not give me
a divorce.

Sleeptalk

Our dreams rise above our heads
& embrace

They ride together
in the ghostly trains of light
which streak across the ceiling

We sleep in their wake

A thin river of slime
joins our snail-mouths

Our eyelids twitch
the Morse codes
of our dreams

Our fingers clutch & unclutch
at the darkness

Palm upward to the stars
mouths shaping zeros
to the silence

Your penis rising
to conduct
your dreams

My moving tongue
still singing to itself

Hook

Nights we spend apart
I am at the bottom of a lake
with my loneliness.
Even a fishhook
would taste good.
I throw myself a line.
I write.

Night terrors come back.
I am four.
There is a man under the bed
who holds his breath
so I will think he's dead.
I know he's cheating
& I hold mine too.
We wait each other out.

Last gasp.
The water fills my lungs.
WOMAN KILLED BY DROWNING IN HER DREAMS.

At the bottom of the world
where books dissolve,
when pencils turn to salt,
where Venice sinks
under the weight
of stolen gold,
the blind fish bump me
& I turn to them.

I speak their silent thoughts
before I sleep.

Three

The best lovers
think constantly of death.
It keeps them honest.
It causes them to make love all night,
avoiding sleep.

We made love all night—
we three.
You & me
& that death's head
which slept between us.
The third impression on our pillow
was death itself—
& I smoothed back your mustache
in the direction from which
it had grown.

All night you drank from me.
The light was bone white,
moon white, white as gravestones.
The sheets were limestone,
the blankets marble shrouds
& in the morning
we lay there quite as numb
as a sarcophagus king
& queen.

What a loving corpse you were!
I have known living men
to be much, much colder.
Being dead,
we needed so much heat—

that we rubbed each other's flints
& made blue sparks.

I think how valiantly we fought off sleep,
& of your skin
like worn-down marble.

I think especially of your gentleness.
Death also can be thanked
for that.

For a Marriage

(*seven years old, just beginning*)

After we had torn out
each other's ribs
& put them back—

after we had juggled thigh bones
& knee caps,
& tossed each other's skulls at friends,

after we had sucked
each other's blood
& spat it out,

after we had sucked
each other's blood
& swallowed it
licking our lips—

after the betrayals
& imagined betrayals—

after you left me in the snow
& I left you in the rain
& we both came back—

after staying together
out of lust
& out of fear
& out of laziness—

we find ourselves
entangled in each other's arms,

grown into each other
like Siamese twins,
embedded in each other
like ingrown toenails,

& for the first time
wanting each other
only.

IV/SLEEPING WITH DEATH

*. . . melancholia is about as happy a state
as any other, I suppose.*

ZELDA FITZGERALD

*I sing of autumn and the falling fruit
and the long journey towards oblivion.*

*The apples falling like great drops of dew
to bruise themselves an exit from themselves.*

D. H. LAWRENCE

The Prisoner

The cage of myself clamps shut.
My words turn the lock.

I am the jailor rattling the keys.
I am the torturer's assistant
who nods & smiles
& pretends not
to be responsible.

I am the clerk who stamps
the death note
affixing the seal, the seal, the seal.

I am the lackey who "follows orders."
I have not got the authority.

I am the visitor
who brings a cake, baked
with a file.

Pale snail,
I wave between the bars.
I speak of rope with the hangman.
I chatter of sparks & currents
with the electrician.
Direct or alternating,
he is beautiful.

I flatter him.
I say he turns me on.

I tell the cyanide capsules
they have talent —

& may fulfill themselves someday.
I read the warden's awful novel
& recommend a publisher.
I sleep with the dietitian
who is hungry.
I sleep with the hangman
& reassure him
that he is a good lover.

I am the ideal prisoner.

I win prizes on my conduct.
They reduce my sentence.
Now it is only 99 years
with death like a dollop
of whipped cream at the end.
I am so grateful.

No one remembers
that I constructed this jail
& peopled its cells.
No one remembers my blueprints
& my plans,
my steady hammering,
my dreams of fantastic escapes.

& even I,
patiently writing away,
my skin yellowing
like the pages of old paperbacks,
my hair turning gray,
cannot remember the first crime,
the crime
I was born for.

The Lure of the Open Window

in memory of Joel Lieber

> *Truth has very few friends and those few are suicides.*
> ANTONIO PORCHIA

The mouth of the night is open.
It wants to eat me.
It says the stars are lonely for me.
It lures me
with a faint wind
like a song.

This window
is the exit of the world.
Beyond it hover
my friends who have stepped off the earth,
out of themselves.
Like beginning swimmers,
they are treading air.

Why does the window
sing to me that way?

At the bottom of the pit
are alley cats & bottle glass
not truth.

Twenty windy stories down,
would I become
wholly myself?

The window hisses.

It is trying to blow out
this poem.

In the Skull

Is there no way out of the mind?
SYLVIA PLATH

Living in a death's head,
peering at life through its eyeholes,
she wondered why she could see only death,
why the landscape of clouds & mountains
looked to her
like the profiles of giant corpses
lying across
the horizon.

She lived in the skull.
She had always lived in the skull.
She kept it tidy.
She swept the floor of the jaw.
She dusted the ridge of the nose.
She rubbed
the nonexistent windows of the eyes
until they shone
like air.
Then she cooked lunch
& rested
on a molar.

Beyond the glittering rows of teeth
she saw the world:
everyone eating or being eaten.
She longed for a lover
to share her house & food
& make her feel alive.

Thirteen Lines for a Childless Couple

Because they thought always of the world ending
because he feared the whiplash of his father's sperm
because she feared the carriages & diapers
because she feared the splitting of her self
because she feared the world rushing in
because he studied little children

they never had children

Their child waited on skis at the top of a green hill
for the snowfall of his father's sperm

They huddled in the ski lodge drinking tea
& studying the cloud configurations

Eventually they died there

& the snow covered them

The End of the World

I am writing to you from the end of the world.
HENRI MICHAUX

Here, at the end of the world,
the flowers bleed
as if they were hearts,
the hearts ooze a darkness
like india ink,
& poets dip their pens in
& they write.

"Here, at the end of the world,"
they write,
not knowing what it means.
"Here, where the sky nurses on black milk,
where the smokestacks feed the sky,
where the trees tremble in terror
& people come to resemble them. . . ."

Here, at the end of the world,
the poets are bleeding.
Writing & bleeding
are thought to be the same;
singing & bleeding
are thought to be the same.

Write us a letter!
Send us a parcel of food!
Comfort us with proverbs or candied fruit,
with talk of one God.
Distract us with theories of art
no one can prove.

Here at the end of the world
our heads are empty,
& the wind walks through them
like ghosts
through a haunted house.

Waiting

It is boring, this waiting for death.
Some days, the wind feathers your hair
& you open your mouth
on a wafer of sky
& you think of death as a book
with blue pages
which you will write.

You will write it by erasing
letter by letter
each word,
each endless day.

Meanwhile the boredom,
the vulgar fat novel:
your life.
Waiting for the baby to be born.
Waiting for the cast to come off,
& scribbling little poems on the plaster.

Where is the archway?
Where is the Tiepolo sky?
Where are the angels & putti?
Where is the life you are so afraid to lose?

Seminar

for Mark Strand

They are the clean boys from the Midwest
who come to New York
with pennies on their tongues
to pay the piper.

They open their mouths & money tumbles out
this ought to be
negotiable for poems
but it is not.

Oh they are glib as pockets full of change
& all have girlfriends
& all turn on
& all get laid two times a week, at least,
& write about it.

They bring their poems to the man
who's slept with death,
& are baffled
when he laughs.

The Universal Explicator

The Universal Explicator
hums softly to itself
the names of dreams
separates the hungers
sets them against each other

The Universal Explicator
grinds out bullets with its bowels
speeches with its mouths
air pollution
from every pore

The Universal Explicator
even makes love
with a choice of dildoes
simultaneously makes war
simultaneously talks peace

The Universal Explicator
gives fellowships to bombs
& defense contracts to poets

A man once tried to murder it
His bullets boomeranged
& shot him dead
The Universal Explicator
canonized him instantly

The Universal Explicator
is tiny & fits
in the palm of your soul
If cornered will explode
inside you

The Other Side of the Page

I pass to the other side of the page.
BABLO NERUDA

On the other side of the page
where the lost days go,
where the lost poems go,
where the forgotten dreams
breaking up like morning fog,
go
go
go

I am preparing myself for death.

I am teaching myself emptiness:
the gambler's hunger for love,
the nun's hunger for God,
the child's hunger for chocolate
in the brown hours
of the dark.

I am teaching myself love:
the lean love of marble
kissed away by rain,
the cold kisses of snow crystals
on granite grave markers,
the soul kisses of snow
as it melts in the spring.

On the other side of the page
I lie making a snow angel
with the arcs
of my arms.

I lie like a fallen skier
who never wants to get up.

I lie with my poles, my pens
flung around me in the snow
too far to reach.

The snow seeps
into the hollows of my bones
& the calcium white of the page
silts me in like a fossil.

I am fixed in my longing for speech,
I am buried in the snowbank of my poems,
I am here where you find me

dead

on the other side of the page.

From the Country of Regrets

Those who live by the word will die listening.
DELMORE SCHWARTZ

It is a country where you can touch nothing: the food, the toilets, the people. The flies are everywhere. You come with your pockets stuffed with money, but there's nothing you can buy for fear of contamination, and nothing you can let touch you.

You enter a hotel with a central court. White plaster nymphs and cherubs in the fountain. Blue and yellow walls with white icing. Palms, ferns, growing out of white plaster planters. Servants sliding around noiselessly as if on invisible ballbearings. Fans turning overhead. The constant continuo of the fountain in the central court. But the statues are sugar. Gradually, the water erodes them and they crumble and fall into the fountain. The fountain crumbles and falls into itself. The whole court dissolves. Next, it begins to dissolve the hotel and the guests, who are also made of sugar. The hawks circle and circle overhead, but they are not interested in melted sugar.

(Directions to the Ruins)

Where is the gate?
> It is a mouth with a tongue
> It is the curled tongue
> of the rain god

Where is the door?

> Under the eyes
> Behind the teeth
> kissed with moss

Where is the roof?

> Over the breasts
> Under the sky
> ruined

Where is the floor?

> Fragments
> A mosaic of a dolphin
> The lost poems of the dolphin minstrels

Where are the birds?

> Under the eaves
> Under the stones
> gone

Where is the altar?

> Under the throat
> Pitted with rain
> slick with blood

Where is the tower?

> Between your legs
> Above the hill
> falling

Where is the well?

> Filled with the bones of girls
> with gold   with blood
> dry

Where is the tomb?
                    Follow the signs
                    Across the river
                    above you

The taxis in this country are ancient American cars. They start with a death rattle in the ignition. They puff along producing a great deal of noise and very little motion. Every thrust forward seems an immense effort. On hills, the drivers and passengers have to get out and push. These cabs are usually painted bright red or green. The paint-jobs are amateurish and seem hastily done to conceal the American paint underneath. Even the windshields are painted red or green. Only little slits remain for the drivers to look out. The interiors are covered everywhere possible with transparent red plastic. It hangs down in strips like old wallpaper. Glued to the plastic are amulets of all kinds: blue beads against the evil eye, Infants of Prague, fat-bellied Buddhas, Arabic mottoes, St. Christopher medals, homages to Quetzalcoatl, tiny reproductions of copulating Hindu gods, copies of the Lascaux animals, tiny plastic unicorns, griffins, sea dragons.

It is difficult to communicate with the people because every family speaks a different language, handed down through the generations and kept within the family like an heirloom. There are a few common words which the whole populace shares: words for MOTHER, MOUTH, FOOD, WAR; the verbs for MAKE, STEAL, BEAT, KILL. . . . But even these words have personal family equivalents which people use in their own homes. A complete common language is not necessary because incest is the rule in this country, and children mate with their own parents and never leave home. Their children, in turn, mate with them, and sometimes even with the grandparents when the grandparents are young enough. There are great numbers of deformed people and hemophiliacs as a result, and citizens with no birth defects are regarded with suspicion, as if they had some contagious disease.

(Chant at the Body's Birth-gate or the Nunnery-door)

Into the mouth

> lost lost forever
> & the teeth
> that prison

Into the eyes

> pull down the shades
> the brain still ticks

Into the nose

> hold it
> it stinks

Into the ears

> oh horny for music

Into the breasts

> dry as powdered bone

Into the navel

> flat
> no tunnel

Into the anus

> cities will die there

Into the cunt

> The cave of the mother
> let me lie down there
> rest
> let me rest

Tourists arrive in the country expecting a pleasant vacation, but within a few days, they are ready to leave. Generally, they fall prey to terrible diarrhea, or vomiting, or both. They try, despite their illness, to visit the great landmarks: The Temple of the Club-footed Virgin, The Cathedral of the Ebony Hermaphrodite, The Triumphal Arch built by King Akiliomoatli, who was born without arms or legs and invented a kind of primitive wheelchair called "doabo" which many citizens still use. But sightseeing is soon made impossible by the constant bouts of diarrhea and the fact that public toilets are either very scarce or contaminated. A few enterprising citizens have made themselves rich by building toilet booths near the main public attractions and charging exorbitant rates to desperate victims. The people who have gotten rich this way are both admired for their shrewdness and looked upon with contempt by the rest of the populace—rather the way Jews are looked upon by gentiles in our culture. Often they become quite influential, but they are never allowed full equality in government and civic positions, and from time to time they are purged in pogroms (called, oddly enough, "Regrets"—though it has no connection whatsoever with the English word, and has, in fact, a wholly different etymology). After these pogroms, the toilet booths are confiscated by the State and given to other citizens. These citizens then become part of the hated caste and in a few generations their descendants are purged, and so it goes. Tourists from our own country consider this horrifying and barbaric.

Invariably, tourists decide to leave after less than a week. They try to make plane reservations, but find the hotel staffs sullen and disinterested. The concierges shrug their shoulders and pretend not to understand when the tourists insist they want to leave. They go to the airline offices but find them always closed. They try to call, but none of the telephones work. Finally, in desperation, they pack and go to the airport.

The airport (which one scarcely noticed on arrival) proves to be one smallish room with peeling yellow walls, old American pop music (a woman singing "Yes, We Have No Bananas" and a man singing "Teenie Weenie Bikini" seem to be the only two records), fans turning overhead, and thousands upon thousands of mosquitoes. The wind riffles a five-year-old calendar with pictures of half-naked girls sitting on orange tractors.

A weathered sign labeled INFORMATION INFORMACION IN-FORMAZIONE hangs over what appears to be a counter. On closer inspection, one finds it is a bar, and those glittering objects which promised so much information are really liquor bottles.

An old woman walks by carrying a pillow in a soiled pillowcase. Except for her, everyone is in straw hats and sunglasses and leis and everyone is overburdened with piñatas, cameras, bottles of watered-down scotch, straw baskets, reproductions of ancient amphorae, straw flowers, skin-diving gear, guidebooks, and pornographic postcards showing leathery-skinned peasant women fornicating with bored-looking donkeys before the ruins. Because of the mosquitoes, everyone is scratching ankles, knees, wrists. There is always a high whine in the air around one's ears.

(*The Poem About Ruins*)

It is your life which writes
the poem about ruins

It rises purple
as a plumed serpent
on a jungled coast

Its eyes are green

:

        the veined wings
        of green insects

It worships sun

:

        We are sitting our adolescence out
        here on the damp floor of a tomb

        We lie praying our hands like buried kings
        Moss kisses our genitals & lips

The poem about ruins
is inside us
trembling

:

        It turns our cheeks
        slate blue

        No one,
        it tells us,
        can write it

Blank sun

I rest on the crumbled wall
of Caracalla's Baths

Something has dried the water up!

A butterfly lights on one shoulder wing

A Roman boy
would like to scrub my back

But my head is parched

:

The poem about ruins

We stumble through the labyrinth in Crete

Here Theseus fell
& Ariadne spread her legs
Here jars of honey stood
here jars of oil
a small way off
there stood the jars of bones

Weeds sprouted from the furrows in my brow
Rain pitted all the limestone of my cheeks
The paint washed off as off the Parthenon
My navel filled with earth
We are sifting through the stones
Ephesus, perhaps, or Ostia

Somewhere near some sea

There is a statue of my mother here
My father is the snake twined round her waist

Look down!

We are climbing the Magician's Temple in Uxmal
You cannot count steps up to the sun

We cling because we want to fall
& the poem about ruins
will be lost

Suddenly, everyone is herded into line for Customs and interrogated severely. A number of people are made to pay the last of their money as duty on articles they brought with them. They argue with the officials, but they cannot prove ownership and, in desperation, they pay. When they return to their seats, some girls find that their pornographic postcards have been stolen. They want to complain to the authorities, but cannot remember any of the words for "donkey."

Finally, the plane is heard landing. The passengers all run out to see it taxi up to the gate. It is a sorry specimen: an old propeller plane with only three working engines and no familiar markings. It bears a painted Dodo on its flank and an Eohippus on its somewhat dented tail. Several of the women become hysterical and refuse to board. Children begin to cry. "Teenie Weenie Bikini" is still playing.

The crew walks out smartly. The captain appears to be wearing a black cowboy suit from a 1940s Western, and a black mask, silver spurs and six-shooters. The stewardesses are dressed like dance hall girls of the Old West. They go over to the INFORMATION bar and order double bourbons which they proceed to bolt down. All the passengers watch them as they parade back across the room and out to the plane.

There is much reluctance and shuffling around, but everyone finally boards. The old woman with the pillow is seen boarding last. The mechanics do a vaudeville imitation of checking the engines, but the fact that they are really not doing anything is clear. One propeller is still not working properly. It turns sluggishly. The takeoff is as slow as running in a dream. The plane seems to hover for a long time with its tail grazing the runway, and the tire treads screech at the moment of takeoff. Then, miraculously, the plane is aloft and hovering over the ocean. The seatbelt sign is still on. The pilot's voice is heard over the P.A. system: "Due to mechanical failure, we will crash shortly." The passengers sit riveted to their seats. Some laugh raucously. Others scream for the stewardesses. Others order drinks.

(*Invisible, with Stalled Engines*)

Perhaps we are not sinking
but God is going higher

He is finally invisible

Clouds pass above us
like milk in water

The sky is water

The plane we fly in
is a giant fish
which seems to stand still

But we believe in motion
we believe in the idea of motion

Forward, we say, is where
we are going

Perhaps God is going higher

We are not sinking
We do not believe we are sinking

Some young people are heard begging the stewardess for philosophical explanations. What have they done wrong? Why does evil have to exist? Why does death? Who willed it all? Doesn't the captain have any power over it?

The stewardesses bat their false eyelashes and smile their plastic smiles and ask: "Milk or juice, sir?" Other passengers sit paralyzed, listening for messages in the sound of the engines. They believe their hearts and the engines correspond.

And there in the corner, writing about everyone, trying to separate herself out of the scene, or be above it, or control it, or pretend she dreamed it—am I. I am the one with the open notebook, the one who lost her pornographic postcards, the one with thousands of mosquito bites behind each knee. Nothing bad can happen to me. I am only collecting material. I am making notes: on hell, on heaven.

It seems as though we have been waiting hours for the crash, but this may be an illusion. The stewardesses have not served drinks yet. Perhaps they do not intend to because of the mechanical trouble. One cannot tell. Also, one cannot hear the engines for the singing. Strapped in our seats, suspended above the ill-fitting fragments of our lives, we are singing. There is no place to get to. The sun is setting below the horizons of our eyes, and all our windows seem to be on fire.

To the Reader

At the point X
the point of ignition,
the point where one tick
of the clock
joins with another,
the point where the scratch of the match
bursts into flame—

that is where I begin,
where I open my hand
to the reader
& shake out my cuffs,
where I show my magician's hat
& swear on my life
it is empty.

At the moment of impact,
at blast-off plus one,
my acetylene pencil
is searing my name
on the backs of my lovers,
my fountain pen breaks into blossom . . .
the paper is pooling with rain.

At the stroke of lightning—
when Toledo appears as a gleam
in El Greco's eye—

at the clap of thunder—
when Beethoven goes deaf
& invents the ear—

I am trying to learn
to begin to begin to begin.

The Artist as Housewife/
The Housewife as Artist*

by Erica Jong

God knows it's hard enough to be an artist at all, so why make a fetish about sex? The future's a mouth. Death's got no sex. The artist, propelled by her horror of death, and some frantic energy which feels half like hunger, half like hot pants, races forward (she hopes) in a futile effort to outrun time, knowing all the while that the race is rigged, doomed, and ridiculous. The odds are with the house.

Being an artist of any sex is such a difficult business that it seems almost ungenerous and naïve to speak of the special problems of the woman artist. The problems of becoming an artist are the problems of selfhood. The reason a woman has greater problems becoming an artist is because she has greater problems becoming a self. She can't believe in her existence past thirty. She can't believe her own voice. She can't see herself as a grown-up human being. She can't leave the room without a big wooden *pass*.

This is crucial in life but even more crucial in art. A woman can go on thinking of herself as a dependent little girl and still get by, if she sticks to the stereotyped roles a woman is supposed to play in our society. Frau Doktor. Frau Architect. Mrs. George Blank. Mrs. Harry Blank. Harold's mother. Mother of charge plates, blank checks, bankbooks; insurance beneficiary, fund raiser, den

*This article first appeared in *Ms.*, December, 1972.

mother, graduate student, researcher, secretary. . . . As long as she goes on taking orders, as long as she doesn't have to tell herself what to do, and be accountable to herself for finishing things. . . . But an artist takes orders only from her inner voice and is accountable only to herself for finishing things. Well, what if you have no inner voice, or none you can distinguish? Or what if you have three inner voices and all three of them are saying conflicting things? Or what if the only inner voice which you can conjure up is male because you can't really conceive of authority as soprano?

Just about the most common complaint of talented women, artists manqué, women who aspire to be artists, is that they *can't finish things.* Partly because finishing implies being judged—but also because finishing things means being grown up. More important, it means possibly succeeding at something. And success, for women, is always partly failure.

Don't get a doctorate because then you'll never find a husband.

Don't be too successful or men will be scared of you.

The implication is always that if you're a success with your brain (or talent or whatever), you'll be a failure with your cunt (or womb or whatever). Success at one end brings failure at the other (Edna St. Vincent Millay's candle notwithstanding). No wonder women are ambivalent about success. Most of them are so ambivalent, in fact, that when success seems imminent they go through the most complex machinations to ward it off. Very often they succeed, too.

The main problem of a poet is to raise a voice. We can suffer all kinds of kinks and flaws in a poet's work except lack of authenticity. Authenticity is a difficult thing to define, but roughly it has to do with our sense of the poet as a *mensch*, a human being, an *author* (with the accent on authority). Poets arrive at authenticity in very different ways. Each poet finds her own road by walking it—sometimes backward, sometimes at a trot. To achieve authenticity you have to know who you are and approximately why. You have to know yourself not only as defined by the roles you play but also as a creature with an inner life, a creature built around an inner darkness. Because women are always encouraged to see themselves as role players and helpers ("helpmate" as a synonym for "wife" is illuminating here), rather than as separate beings, they find it hard to grasp this authentic sense of self. They have too many easy cop-outs.

Probably men are just as lazy and would cop out if they could. Surely men have similar and very crushing problems of selfhood and identity. The only difference is that men haven't got the built-in escape from identity that women have. They can't take refuge in being Arnold's father or Mr. Betty Jones. Women not only can, but are encouraged to, are often forbidden not to, are browbeaten into believing that independence is "castrating," "phallic," or "dykey."

It's not that women lack the inner darkness—one might almost argue that women are ideally suited to be artists because of their built-in darkness, and the mysteries they are privy to—but women don't explore that darkness as men do. And in art, the exploration is all. Everyone has talent. What is rare is the courage to follow the talent to the dark place where it leads.

Of course, it's also a question of trust. Katherine Anne Porter said that becoming a writer was all a question of learning to trust yourself, to trust your own voice. And that's just what most women can't do. That's why they are always seeking someone to dictate to them, someone to be their perennial graduate student adviser, someone to give them gold stars for being good girls.

Naming is the crucial activity of the poet; and naming is a form of self-creation. In theory, there's nothing wrong with the woman's changing names for each new husband, except that often she will come to feel that she has no

name at all. (All men are mirrors. Which one will she look into today?) So her first name, her little girl name is the only one which winds up sounding real to her. Erica.
Erica X.
My father (death) has come to get me.
May I please leave the room?
I have a sleep-over date.

If women artists often elect to use their maiden (or even maternal) names, it's in a sort of last-ditch attempt to assert an unchanging identity in the face of the constant shifts of identity which are thought in our society to constitute femininity. Changing names all the time is only symbolic of this. It's only disturbing because it mirrors the inner uncertainty.

To have ten identities (wife, mother, mistress, cook, maid, chauffeur, tutor, governess, banker, poet?) is really to have none—or at least none you can believe in. You always feel like a dilettante. You always feel fragmented. You always feel like a little girl. Characteristically, women think of themselves as first names (children): men think of themselves as last names (grown-ups).

And what about "writing like a man" and the word "poetess" (which has come to be used like the word "nigrah")? I know of no woman writer who hasn't confessed the occasional temptation to send her work out under a masculine nom de plume, or under initials, or under the "protection" of some male friend or lover. I know women who can never finish a novel because they insist on making their narrators men, and women poets who are hung up on "androgynous poems" in an attempt to fool the first readers (often self-hating women like themselves).

But sex—it seems so obvious one shouldn't even have to say it—is a part of identity, and if a writer's problem is to find her human identity, only more so, then how can she manage this while concealing her sex?

She can't.

I knew I wanted to be a writer from the time I was ten or eleven and, starting then, I attempted to write stories. The most notable thing about these otherwise not very memorable stories was that the main character was always male. I never tried to write about women and I never thought anyone would be interested in a woman's point of view. I assumed that what people wanted to hear was how men thought women were, not what women themselves thought they were. None of this was quite conscious, though. I wrote about boys in the same way a black child draws blond hair (like mine) on the faces in her sketchbook.

Yet I did not think of myself as self-hating, and it was only years later (when I was in my late twenties) that I realized how my self-hatred had always paralyzed me as a writer. In high school, I thought I loved myself and I was full of dreams of glory. At fourteen, I declared myself a feminist, read bits and pieces of *The Second Sex*, and ostentatiously carried the book around. I talked about never wanting to marry—or at the very least not until I was thirty (which then must have seemed like old age to me). But for all my bravado, whenever I sat down to write, I wrote about men. Why? I never asked myself why.

It may also be relevant to point out that until I was twenty or so, all the characters I invented had WASP names—names like Mitch Mitchell, Robert Robertson, Elizabeth Anderson, Bob Briggs, Duane Blaine. Names like the ones you saw in school readers. Names like the ones you heard on radio soap operas. None of the kids I grew up with had such names. They were all Weinbergers and Hamburgers and Blotniks and Briskins and Friskins. There were even some Singhs and Tsangs and Wongs and Fongs. There were even some McGraths and

Kennedys and McCabes. The Mitchells in my high school class could be counted on the digits of one severely frost-bitten foot, or one leprous hand. But they were in all my stories.

This only proves that one's own experience is less convincing than the cultural norm. In fact, one has to be strong indeed to *trust* one's own experience. Children characteristically lack this strength. And most women, in our culture, are encouraged to remain children. I know two little girls whose mother is a full-time practicing physician who works a very long day and works at home. The children see the patients come and go. They know their mother is a doctor, and yet one of them returned from nursery school with the news that men were doctors and women had to be nurses. All her mother's reasoning and all the child's own experience could not dissuade her.

So, too, with my feelings about writers. I spent my whole bookish life identifying with writers and nearly all the writers who mattered were men. Even though there were women writers, and even though I read them and loved them, they did not seem to *matter*. If they were good, they were good in *spite* of being women. If they were bad, it was *because* they were women. I had, in short, internalized all the dominant cultural stereotypes. And the result was that I could scarcely even imagine a woman as an author. Even when I read Boswell, it was with him that I identified and not with the women he knew. Their lives seemed so constricted and dull compared with his dashing around London. I, too, loved wordplay and clever conversation. I, too, was a clown. I, too, was clever and a bit ridiculous. I *was* Boswell. The differences in our sexes honestly never occurred to me.

So, naturally, when I sat down to write, I chose a male narrator. Not because I was deluded that I was a man—but because I was very much a woman, and being a woman means, unfortunately, believing a lot of male definitions (even when they cause you to give up significant parts of your own identity).

Of course there were women writers, too, but that didn't seem to change anything. There was Dorothy Parker, whose stories I had by heart and whose bittersweet verses I'd recite whenever I could find a baffled adolescent boy who'd listen. There was Edna St. Vincent Millay, whose sonnets I had memorized from my mother's old, leather-bound, gold-tooled, tear-stained editions (with the crushed violets between the pages). There was Simone de Beauvoir, who seemed so remotely intellectual and French. There was Colette, who wrote of a baffling theatrical world of lesbian love whose significance eluded me then. And there was Virginia Woolf, whose style, at that point in my life, was too rich for my blood.

Except for Parker and Millay (whom I mythicized as much as read), it was to the male writers that I had to go. I even learned about women from them—trusting implicitly what they said, even when it implied my own inferiority.

I had learned what an orgasm was from D. H. Lawrence, disguised as Lady Chatterley.

I learned from him that all women worship "the Phallos"—as he so quaintly spelled it. (For years I measured my orgasms against Lady Chatterley's and wondered what was *wrong* with me. It honestly never occurred to me that Lady Chatterley's creator was a man, and perhaps not the best judge of female orgasms. It honestly never occurred to me to trust myself or other women.) I learned from Shaw that women never can be artists. I learned from Dostoevski that they have no religious feeling. I learned from Swift and Pope that they have too much religious feeling (and therefore can never be quite rational). I learned from Faulkner that they are earth-mothers and at one with the moon and the tide and the crops. I learned from Freud that they have deficient superegos and are ever "incomplete" because they lack the one thing in this world worth having: a penis.

I didn't really become an avid reader of poetry until college. The modern poets I loved best then were Yeats and Eliot, Auden and Dylan Thomas. Diverse as they were, they had in common the assumption of a male viewpoint and a masculine voice, and when I imitated them, I tried to sound either male or neuter. Despite Emily Dickinson, poetry, for me, was a masculine noun. It came as a revelation to discover contemporary women poets like Anne Sexton, Sylvia Plath, and Denise Levertov, and to realize that strong poetry could be written out of the self that I had systematically (though perhaps unconsciously) repressed. And it was not until I allowed the femaleness of my personality to surface in my work that I began to write anything halfway honest.

I remember the year when I began to write seriously, when I threw out all my college poems and began again. What I noticed most persistently about my earliest poems was the fact that they did not engage my individuality very deeply. I had written clever poems about Italian ruins and villas, nightingales and the graves of poets—but I had tried always to avoid revealing myself in any way. I had assumed a stock poetic voice and a public manner. It was as though I disdained myself, felt I had no *right* to have a self. Obviously an impossible situation for a poet.

How did this change? It's hard to chronicle in detail because the change was gradual and I can't retrace each step. I was living in Europe in a kind of cultural and intellectual isolation. I was part of no consciousness-raising group. I was part of no writing seminar. Yet gradually I managed to raise my own consciousness as a poet. The main steps were these: first I owned up to being Jewish, urban, and American; then I owned up to my femaleness.

It was in Germany that I first set myself the task of writing as if my life depended on it (and of writing every day). For an atheistic New York Jew who had been raised to feel as indifferent to religion as possible, Germany was an overwhelming experience. Suddenly I felt as paranoid as a Jew in hiding during the Nazi period. For the first time I began to confess to my primal terror, to my sense of being a victim. I began to delve into my own fears and fantasies, and finally I began to write about these things. Little by little, I was able to strip away the disguises. I was able to stop disdaining myself. I was able to stop feeling that what I was (and therefore what I had to write about) must, of necessity, be unimportant.

From persecuted Jew to persecuted woman is not a very long step. When you begin to open up your own sense of vulnerability and make poetry of it, you are on your way to understanding your femaleness as well. That was the progression for me. First I confessed to being a victim. Then I identified with victims. Finally, I was able to cast off the mask of the WASP male oppressor which I (and my writing) had worn for so long.

From then on, it was just a question of burrowing deeper and deeper. I no longer had anything to hide. Once I confessed to my vulnerability, I was able to explore it, and from that everything followed. I stopped writing about ruins and nightingales. I was able to make poetry out of the everyday activities of my life: peeling onions, a trip to the gynecologist, a student demonstration, my own midnight terrors and dreams—all the things I would have previously dismissed as trivial.

Because of my own history, I think women poets have to insist on their right to write like women. Where their experience of the world is different, women writers ought to reflect that difference. They ought to feel a complete freedom about subject matter. But most important, our definition of femininity has to change. As long as femininity is associated with ruffles and flourishes and a lack of directness and honesty, women artists will feel a deep sense of ambivalence about their own femaleness. In a culture where the word *woman* is a synonym for *second-rate*, there's no mystery about why women want to "write like men."

In cultural life, as elsewhere, women are damned if they do and damned if they don't. They are often paralyzed and afraid to write because they feel their experience is trivial, yet if they write outside of their experience, they are condemned as unauthentic. No matter how great their achievement, they are always called women artists rather than artists. No wonder they are so afraid to write, and having written are so afraid to submit their work for display or judgment. Even their greatest successes are tinged with failure. They are never praised without being patronized. Their jacket photographs are reviewed instead of their books.

When I was in college, I remember listening (and growing increasingly depressed) as a visiting writer went on and on about how women couldn't possibly be authors. Their experience was too limited, he said. They didn't know blood and guts and fucking whores and puking in the streets, he growled. At the time this silly cliché made me miserable. How could a girl hope to be a writer unless she had a history more lurid than that of Moll Flanders? (It never occurred to me then that this let out most men, too.) It was the old Hemingway routine. The writer as tough guy. The writer as Tarzan crossed with King Kong. Naturally, if you believed that *machismo* garbage, you had to believe that (most) women couldn't be authors. And certainly men who had empathy with women (or indeed with *any*one) were excluded, too.

A few years later, when I got to know Neruda's elemental odes about lemons and artichokes, and Ponge's prose poems about soap and seashells and oysters, and William Carlos Williams's red wheelbarrow, and Gary Snyder's essay about the poet as tender of the earth household, I was able to reconsider the parallels between the poet and the housewife and find the two far more similar than any growling male writer of the Tarzan-King Kong school would want to believe. The trouble with the phallic-warmongering-whoring image of the damned, doomed artist was not only that it so often backfired (literally in Hemingway's case, figuratively in the case of others), but that it was essentially so destructive and so false. It came out of a sensibility which can only be called imperialist: man against nature and man against woman. What was needed was a different concept of potency (and *poetency*) and a different concept of the artist. Perhaps all artists were, in a sense, housewives: tenders of the earth household. Perhaps a nurturing sensibility had never been more needed. Besides, it was the inner experience, not the outer one, which was crucial. One of the things which make a poet a poet is the ability to see the world in a grain of sand or eternity in a wildflower (or an onion). As Valéry says, "It is with our own substance that we imagine and create a stone, a plant, a movement, an *object*: any object is perhaps only the beginning of ourselves."

Like blacks, women will have to learn first to love their own bodies; and women poets will have to learn to write about their bodies. Their breasts: those two blind animals with painted eyes. Their cunts: those furry deaf-mutes speaking a red tongue. The astounding royal purple of their blood. It will not do to continue to confuse the pen with the penis. Despite all the cultural stereotypes which equate femininity with second-rateness, women artists will have to learn to explore their own femininity and to define its true nature. Just as male artists will have to confront their envy of women (which often takes the form of asserting that women can't be artists), women artists will have to confront their own bodies and the symbolic implications of their bodies. It seems to me not accidental that two of the most prolific and courageous contemporary women poets (Anne Sexton and Denise Levertov) long ago attempted to write about their bodies and never attempted to conceal that they were women.

Nor does it seem accidental that one of the few female artists to fully explore her own anger at being a woman (Sylvia Plath) could never return from that exploration. Plath's extraordinary burst of creativity after childbirth bears witness to the kind of power hidden in women if only it could be tapped. We can't any longer doubt its existence. Our problem is how to tap it without going mad.

The pseudocompliment ("you write like a man"), and the contempt in which the term "poetess" is held, both attest to the fact that all of us (even feminists) continue to regard masculinity as a standard of excellence. We still use the word "feminine" as if it were synonymous with foolish, frivolous, and silly. In his sniggeringly sexist introduction to *Ariel*, Robert Lowell "compliments" Sylvia Plath (who is too dead to hear) by saying that she is "hardly a person at all, or a woman, certainly not another 'poetess'. . . ." No wonder Lady Lazarus rises out of the ash with her red hair—"And I eat men like air."

Note also the Kirkus-service blurb on the back of Marge Piercy's second book of poems: "Angry, alive, loving, real poetry: not feminine, but powerfully female." As if "feminine" and "real poetry" were opposites.

Since authenticity is the key to everything, it seems particularly fatal for a woman artist to become a surrogate male. Nearly all the women poets of our time who have succeeded in becoming individual voices know this. They explore the fact of being female and go beyond it, but they never deny it. Of course, they pay dearly for this in condescending reviews (which seldom fail to disparage their sex in some way or other), and their reputations are somehow seldom taken as seriously as those of male poets of the same (or lesser) quality. But at least they go on writing and publishing; they go on working. Yet they are so pitifully few in number! For the handful of Levertovs, Plaths, Richs, Piercys, Swensons, Kizers, Sextons

—there must be thousands of talented women, sitting on unfinished books, wondering how to make themselves sound unfeminine.

I think as we become more aware of the deep relationship between poetry and ecology, we will begin to revalue the female sensibility in poetry (and in all the arts). We will begin to value the exploration of femaleness (as many ancient civilizations did) rather than to reject it.

But if there's too much male chauvinism in literature and in the literary world, the answer to it is not female chauvinism. Beyond the initial freedom women writers need (of allowing themselves to write like women), there's the greater goal of the mature artist: to become artistically bisexual.

Virginia Woolf points out that the process of developing as an artist means at some point transcending gender. It means having empathy for both sexes, partaking of both halves of humanity and reconciling them in one's work.

At just about this point I anticipate a howl of outrage about my use of the words "male" and "female" and my assumption that there is such a thing as a "female sensibility" in poetry or elsewhere. Unfortunately, the terms male and female have become so loaded and politicized, so laden with old prejudices, that they are almost useless for purposes of communication. We don't know what masculine really means, nor what feminine really means. We assume them to be opposites and we may not even be right about that. Yet we are stuck with these words. They are deeply embedded in language and in our minds (which language in part helped to shape). What shall we do with masculine and feminine? Does it do anyone any good just to pretend that they don't exist?

Gradually, we will redefine them. Gradually, society will change its false notions of male and female, and perhaps they will cease to be antitheses. Gradually, male experience and female experience will cease to be so disparate, and then maybe we will not have to worry about women understanding their own self-hatred as a prerequisite to authentic creative work. But what are we to do in the meantime? In our society, men and women still *do* have different life patterns and different experiences. Shouldn't each sex be permitted an authentic expression of its own experience?

Luckily, the artist has an answer. The artist is not finally male or female, but both at once. It is as though the artist were one of those African votive figurines which have breasts, a pregnant belly, and a penis. I think of Leopold Bloom giving birth, of Orlando changing sexes with the centuries. I think of the artist as a mental hermaphrodite, or as a shaman who exploits sexuality in order to get beyond sexuality. The artist starts by exploring her/his particular sexual identity, but this is only the beginning. It is only a necessary way inward. Once women writers are able to write freely about being women, they will be able to write freely about being human. They will be able to explore the world with the confidence that it really belongs to them—just as male writers have always done.

Women artists cannot escape exploring their own sexuality, because the connection between sex and inspiration is intimate. They are both forms of intense energy. They connect and correspond. The relationship between the artist and the Muse is a sexual relationship in which it is impossible to tell who is fucking and who is being fucked. If sex and creativity are often seen by dictators as subversive activities, it's because they lead to the knowledge that you own your own body (and with it your own voice), and that's the most revolutionary insight of all.

Writing a First Novel*

By Erica Jong

I'm supposed to speak today on "writing a first novel," and the trouble is—I don't believe there *is* such a thing as a first novel.

"First novel" is one of those meaningless reviewers' categories, like "black novel," "Jewish novel," or "feminist novel." One might as well speak of "three novels of two hundred pages each" or "two novels by former residents of Great Neck" or "four novels which happened to be published on April 26th . . ." or "three novels by writers whose first name is John." In fact, a friend and I have a standing joke about the "John School" of novelists: John Cheever, John Updike, John Gardner, John Leonard, John O'Hara. . . . Grouping first novels together is quite as ridiculous as that, and so too is the popular practice of grouping writings by women in reviews.

Portrait of the Artist as a Young Man was a "first novel" and so was *Valley of the Dolls. Mashenka* was Nabokov's "first novel," but had he not published an *eleventh* novel entitled *Lolita,* no one here would ever have read it.

Reviewers will persist in calling certain books "first novels," I'm sure, but that's for their own convenience rather than for the sake of literature. The danger for the young writer lies in confusing the reviewer's handle with some truth about the creative process. It must be con-

*This article was first published in *Twentieth Century Literature*, Vol. 20, No. 1, October, 1974. It was presented as a lecture at Hofstra University in April, 1974, and in a somewhat different form at the American Booksellers Convention in Washington, D. C., 1974.

stantly borne in mind that the two are utterly unrelated.

Any number of writers produce three, four, five, six novels before novel number seven gets published and is reviewed as a "first novel." Updike once said in an interview that for every novel he'd published, he'd scrapped another. People are forever asking writers "how long" it took them to finish a given book. The question is natural enough, but how on earth does one answer it? Do you count as "writing time" the years you spent evolving to the point of being able to sit at your desk for more than five minutes at a time? Do you count the years of false starts—novels you wrote ten, twenty, thirty, forty, fifty, sixty, seventy, eighty, ninety, or one hundred pages of and then abandoned in despair? Do you count those other abortive books which you never showed anyone (not even a friend) and which you cannibalized for poems, stories, other novels? Do you count the years of head-shrinking in which you spoke about the tremors that seized you whenever you came face to face with a blank page?

By these criteria, *Fear of Flying* took at least eight years to write—and possibly my whole life. The draft which was finally published was about two years in the writing, but there was a long history before that.

It's a difficult history to reconstruct because memory fictionalizes and distorts the past, and both vanity and false modesty get in the way. One tends to forget some of the most painful difficulties (pain is always hard to remember) and to overstress others. "The remembered event becomes a fiction—a structure made to accommodate certain feelings"—as Jerzy Kosinski says, and this is true even when the remembered event is the creation of a fiction.

So let me try to remember as best I can. . . .

I had always wanted to write fiction—and even when I was writing poetry (and publishing poetry)—I was a closet fiction writer. But I never showed the fiction to anyone because I was afraid. Poetry was not the language of the land. No matter how direct and painful its subject, it was not likely to be read by many people. That provided a measure of protection. Besides, in poetry, one was masked by metaphor, by technique, by the creation of personae who spoke in one's place. And there was so much sheer work-play: wooing "Dame Philology" (as Auden calls it). So I showed my poems (and published them) while I kept my fiction secret.

I think I suspected that ours was a particularly difficult time for fiction—a time in which fiction was changing. The boundaries between fiction and memoir seemed perilously thin, and even the boundaries between fiction and poetry meant very little in great writers like Joyce and Lawrence and Borges. In other great writers like Colette, Proust, Jean Rhys—categories like autobiography and fiction were wholly irrelevant—as they are in poetry. Colette wrote mock memoirs—novels in which she selected and rearranged events from her own life and shaped them—not as they had happened to her in reality, but as they had to happen in the world of art. We think of this interweaving of autobiography and fiction as peculiarly modern, but, in fact, it is part of the old tradition of the English novel. The earliest novels in England (which purported to be the true confessions of famous criminals) were presented to the public as fact. The interweaving of fact and fiction is one of the great themes of the novel and is not a modern invention at all. It just depends on which portion of the tradition you choose to look at.

Though I loved the perfectly wrought novels of E. M. Forster and Elizabeth Bowen, I began to feel that *that* was a kind of novel I could not use as the frame for my experience of life—or at least not yet. In poetry I could be pared down, honed, minimal. In the novel what I wanted was excess, digression, rollicking language, energy, and poetry. *Tristram Shandy* rather than a well-wrought urn. Henry Miller or Colette rather than Forster or Bowen.

I also noticed that the books I read with most pleasure and most avid attention were often memoirs or novels that had the immediacy of memoirs. Even in writers I wholly loved, I tended to prefer the first-person novels to the third-person ones: in Bellow, for example, I preferred Henderson and Augie March to his third-person novels. I loved the novel that pretended *not* to be a novel, in short —the novel that made you believe it was all spilled truth.

Meanwhile, I was writing, but I was not writing in accordance with my perceptions. I was—like most frightened young writers—avoiding myself. My first attempted "first novel" was a first-person Nabokovian melodrama about a young madman who thought he was God. Why Nabokovian? Because I loved Nabokov and had read and reread everything of his—even his mammoth Eugene Onegin translation. Why a *man* as protagonist? Because I never thought anyone would *care* about a woman's fate. All serious novels were about men—weren't they? Despite George Eliot, despite Colette, despite Virginia Woolf—I honestly never questioned this absurdity. It was 1965 and (though I called myself a feminist) I never stopped to ask myself why I felt my protagonists *had* to be male.

My madman novel fell apart after about 150 pages. (Its working title had been *God on West End Avenue*.) It proved too difficult to sustain the madman's viewpoint and also show the things that were happening in the outside, "sane" world. I was stuck inside the head of a mad protagonist and everything had to be seen through his eyes. This finally overwhelmed me. Eventually I put the novel aside. I had learned a lot from it (though I didn't think so at the time), and I would eventually come back to this same madman, seen from the point of view of his wife, in Chapter 12 of *Fear of Flying*. Nobody ever read that early novel but me. Cowardice, perhaps, or maybe prudence.

The next novel I attempted was called *The Man Who Murdered Poets*. Again, the narrator was male (a handy way of avoiding certain basic confrontations with myself), the style Nabokovian, and the theme was the envy wrought by fame. A young male poet, living in Heidelberg (where I was, in fact, living at the time) believes himself a failure and is consumed with envy of a better-known poet, who he believes is his double. He plans to seek him out and murder him in an effort to inherit—magically—his creative powers. I got that far and gave up, having committed about two hundred pages. I knew the book was false. Certain things worked: the descriptions of Germany, the feelings of Americans living in Europe, the parodies of the current poetry scene. But the book lacked life and authenticity. I was not really interested in pretending to be a mad male poet. I knew I had other fish to fry first.

Meanwhile, my poems were changing. I had started out in college writing sonnets and sestinas about unicorns, Venetian paintings, Roman fountains, and the graves of English poets—but now I was beginning to discover that these, too, were evasions for me. My poetry was getting braver. I was no longer writing heroic couplets (as I had in college); I was reading Levertov and Williams, Neruda and Alberti—and trying to learn free verse. I was in psychoanalysis and for the first time was trying to write about my violent feelings about being Jewish in Germany, and my violent feelings about being female in a male-dominated world. I was beginning to be more in touch with my dreams and fantasies. My poems no longer assumed a pseudo-neuter persona. They were frankly female, and that, for the first time, became part of their subject. It had decidedly *not* been important in my early college poems.

When I returned to the United States in 1969, I had a book of poems almost done (or so I thought). That book was to go through three major revisions and housecleanings before emerging in 1971 as *Fruits & Vegetables*. It was really my third book-length manuscript. The first two were buried (gladly). The third was published as my "first book."

Having made this giant step (for me) of publishing a book of poems spoken by a female persona, I returned to my second abortive novel. It was an evasion, I knew, but now I had a publisher who wanted to see it and I hoped, somehow, he'd like it better than I did. So, after delaying for a whole year (and trying to patch it up), I finally showed it to him. He sat on it for a few months and then confirmed what I already knew. It was not authentic. It lacked heart, guts—life, in short. It was clear I was just bursting to write a book about a woman and that was the book we both knew I had to tackle. Almost telepathically, I had begun *Fear of Flying* one week before my conference with my editor.

Not that it was easy. I began *Fear of Flying* with great trepidation. I kept telling myself I was a poet, really, and that if I failed totally I'd still be a poet. All through the first hundred pages of *Fear of Flying*, I was also writing poems at a great rate—some of the poems that went into *Half-Lives*. That winter I put the novel aside to assemble the new poems which had accumulated since *Fruits & Vegetables*—and I found I had a new book—which became *Half-Lives*.

Meanwhile, *Fear of Flying* kept on coming. It wasn't called *Fear of Flying* then. I didn't get the title until I had more than three hundred pages written. And even then I wasn't sure. The book grew, was revised, re-arranged, and kept moving. I showed it to no one—not my agent, not my editor. Certainly not my husband (who was, anyway, reading it in secret, I learned later). I didn't want anyone to read it yet. It was too fragile, too much a five-month-old fetus to live in the air yet.

I wasn't ready to show the book until it was almost seven eighths done. I thought my editor and agent would both hate it because it was so outrageous, so sexually out-spoken, and so literary at the same time. I never *dreamed* it would find a wide audience. It seemed to me the book I *had* to write—whether it was ever published or not. I knew I planned to finish this one, even if only to commit it to a drawer. For the first time I knew I was not evading myself. I was writing as if my life depended on it, and to some extent, it did.

At times, the writing was hell, and at times it was bliss. At times I would grow bored with Isadora and long to be in another consciousness, and at times I would love her and learn from her things I had never known about myself. I sensed that I was doing something new with this book in certain ways and I anticipated great re-sistance. The eroticism that had ultimately been accepted from Henry Miller and D. H. Lawrence and Joyce had *never* been accepted when it came from a woman writer. Women writers were allowed to be sexless angels like Virginia Woolf or Emily Dickinson—but when they wrote of sexuality, they suffered the fate of Violette Leduc. Even Anaïs Nin, the great truth-sayer, recently confessed that when she decided to publish, she omitted the sexual parts of her diary because she had witnessed the fate of Violette Leduc. Sexuality was not permitted for women—and to this day, it still is not permitted in many quarters. Witness this recent review of *Fear of Flying* from liberated England.

With such continual and insistent reference to her cherished valve, Erica Jong's witless heroine looms like a mammoth pudenda, as roomy as the Carlsbad Caverns, luring amorous spelunkers to confusion in her plunging grottoes. On her eighth psychoanalyst and second marriage, Isadora Wing admits to a con-tortion we are not privileged to observe and con-fesses, "I seem to live inside my cunt," which strikes one as a choice as inconvenient as a leaky bedsitter in Elmer's End. Isadora is a journalist, covering an analysts' conference in Vienna and finding some pleasure with an English quack who cheers her up by insulting her. Isadora is a poet as well, and one of her poems, reprinted here by permission, appeared first in *The Beloit Poetry Journal* under the name of Mrs. Jong, who is presumably embarrassed by such awfulness and wishes to dissociate herself from it once and for all. Isadora is also a feminist, interlarding her memoir with grim quotations from Sylvia Plath and Anne Sexton, and tendentious ones from Freud and Rudolf Hess. She says she "wanted to write *War and Peace* or nothing," and having chosen the latter, seems to have settled for the ambition of being gamahuched from here to eternity. But there are problems: "the big problem was how to make your feminism jibe with your unappeasable hunger for male bodies. It wasn't easy."

This crappy novel, misusing vulgarity to the point where it becomes purely foolish, picturing woman as a hapless organ animated by the simplest ridicule, and devaluing imagination in every line (of which "Vienna. The very name is like a waltz" and "Glaciers of grievances which extended far, far beneath the surface of the sea" are but two), represents everything that is to be loathed in American fiction today. It does not have the excuse of humour, nor is its pretence to topicality anything but tedious. That it was written with a grant (gratefully acknowledged on page 5) from the National Endowment for the Arts should surprise no one already familiar with the ways American money is used, though is ample justification for any of us to refuse paying his taxes this year.[1]

[1]Paul Theroux, "Hapless Organ," *New Statesman*, 19 April 1974, p. 554.

In a way, I expected that sort of response all the time I was writing *Fear of Flying*, and I knew I must not capitulate to it. I wanted to write a female picaresque. I had in mind novels like *Tom Jones, Henderson the Rain King, Augie March,* and Henry Miller's *Tropics,* and I saw no reason why the same liberties with language should not belong to women since women take them in life. *Fear of Flying* is not really a very sexy book. It is all about unfulfillment. All that is new about it—if anything—is the explicitness of the *language.* The sexual *acts* in the book are nearly all abortive or unfulfilling, and that was what I intended. It was *meant* to be a saga of unfulfillment, and it was *meant* to challenge the notion that intellectual women must be heads without bodies. Astoundingly enough, the opposition to these self-evident truths continues. Women are supposed to be all brain (for which they are then castigated as narrow) or all earth mother (for which they are then castigated as brainless and bovine). Besides, if we women appropriate woman as our subject, we are not only shocking male (and many female) reviewers, but we are also stealing the favorite subject of male writers—which is: *woman.* No wonder they hate us.

Reviews *are* painful—no matter what sort of front of disdain one puts up—and besides they often represent cash in the bank or books in the bookstore—but one tries to go on. Each book feels, in the writing, like a first book if it is any good at all, and the nature of the writer's craft is perpetual apprenticeship. I would fear for that writer who sits down at his desk feeling like a master. He is likely to be masturbating. One *should* feel frightened, nervous, unsure, and on the verge of perilous discoveries. One *should* be humbled by the dark side of the unconscious and the unpredictability of the creative process. Every book *should* be a first book for every writer, every time.

ABOUT ERICA JONG

Erica Jong was born Erica Mann in New York City and grew up on the Upper West Side. She attended the High School of Music and Art, Barnard College, Columbia University's Graduate Facilities, and the Writing Division of the School of the Arts at Columbia. For a few years, she taught college English at City College of New York, Manhattan Community College, and the University of Maryland's Overseas Division in Heidelberg, Germany. From 1966 to 1969, she lived in Europe and traveled extensively.

Her first published book was *Fruits & Vegetables* (Holt, Rinehart & Winston, 1971). It was far more widely read than the usual first volume of poems and attracted much critical attention. Her next book of poems, *Half-Lives* (Holt, Rinehart & Winston, 1973), won the Alice Faye di Castagnola Award of the Poetry Society of America as well as a writing fellowship from CAPS (the Creative Artists Program Service); and poems in that collection also were awarded the Bess Hokin Prize given by *Poetry* magazine.

In the spring of 1973, Erica Jong received a fellowship from the National Endowment for the Arts for her fiction and poetry. In the fall of 1973, Erica Jong's novel *Fear of Flying* was published to wide critical acclaim. The book appeared on best-seller lists across the country and was hailed by such writers as John Updike, Henry Miller, Elizabeth Janeway, and Hannah Green. The following year it became a paperback phenomenon.

Erica Jong is also a frequent contributor to *Ms.* magazine, and has written reviews and articles for *New York* magazine, *Mademoiselle, Partisan Review, The New York Times Book Review,* and many others. Her poetry and fiction have appeared in numerous magazines such as *The New Yorker, Cosmopolitan, The Paris Review, Poetry, Encounter, The New York Times Magazine, Columbia Forum, Harper's, The New York Quarterly, The Southern Review, Redbook, Ladies Home Journal, Esquire,* etc. She is a much-anthologized poet and is also known for her lively poetry readings at colleges across the country. From 1971 through 1974, she taught a poetry workshop at the Poetry Center of the 92nd Street "Y" in Manhattan. She has a third book of poetry, *Loveroot,* appearing in 1975, and she is at work on another novel as well as a fourth collection of poems.

She has also written the screenplay for the film version of *Fear of Flying* and many essays and articles on women writers such as Colette, Doris Lessing, Adrienne Rich, Sylvia Plath, and Anne Sexton.

More Bestsellers from SIGNET

☐ **IF BEALE STREET COULD TALK by James Baldwin.** A masterpiece about the love between a man and a woman. . . . **The New York Times** called this bestseller "One of the best novels of the year!" A Literary Guild Alternate Selection. (#J6502—$1.95)

☐ **ELIZABETH AND CATHERINE by Robert Coughlin.** For the millions enthralled by **Nicholas & Alexandra,** the glittering lives and loves of the two Russian Empresses who scandalized the world and made a nation . . . "Fascinating!"—The Boston Globe. A Putnam Award Book and a Literary Guild Featured Alternate. (#J6455—$1.95)

☐ **CARRIE by Stephen King.** The psychic terror of **Rosemary's Baby!** The sexual violence of **The Exorcist!** A novel of a girl possessed of a terrifying power . . . "Gory and horrifying . . . you can't put it down!"— **Chicago Tribune** (#E6410—$1.75)

☐ **THE SWARM by Arthur Herzog.** A masterpiece of chilling terror. "For those who relished **The Andromeda Strain,** a suspense story of death and destruction wrought by a new, deadly species of bee."—**Washington Post Book World** (#J6351—$1.95)

☐ **LAST RIGHTS by Marya Mannes.** A brilliant writer makes an eloquent plea for the dying and the right to a dignified death . . . "A book to read and to pass on to others . . . passionate and direct."—**The New York Times** (#W6306—$1.50)

THE NEW AMERICAN LIBRARY, INC.,
P.O. Box 999, Bergenfield, New Jersey 07621

Please send me the SIGNET BOOKS I have checked above. I am enclosing $_____(check or money order—no currency or C.O.D.'s). Please include the list price plus 25¢ a copy to cover handling and mailing costs. (Prices and numbers are subject to change without notice.)

Name_____

Address_____

City_____State_____Zip Code_____
Allow at least 3 weeks for delivery

Have You Read These Bestsellers from SIGNET?